the breakfast book

dorset cereals®

contents

Mudeford Sand Spit, Dorset

Introduction:
In praise of breakfast...

At Dorset Cereals, we love breakfast. We spend our days at our HQ in Poundbury in Dorset creating, tasting and testing our award-winning mueslis, granolas, porridges, flakes and cereal bars, and we only make the recipes that we all agree are the very best.

This book is a celebration of everything we do and make, but also a homage to breakfast itself. Created by our development chef Cheryl Bouchier, the recipes bring together all our favourites, from breakfast bars to fry ups and from smoothies to smoked mackerel kedgeree. Whether you're looking for breakfast on the run or a long lazy Sunday brunch, there is something for everyone.

Are you a skipper?

We've heard that, bizarrely, some people skip breakfast in order to snatch a few extra minutes in bed. Sleep in the kitchen! Nutritionists – and your mother – have been telling you for years that breakfast is the most important meal of the day. Why? Because eating breakfast can ...

- boost your thinking power
- improve your productivity
- maintain your health and well-being
- perhaps even help you to lose weight (although that depends on what you eat)
- make you more attractive (okay – we made that one up, but you should see the people who work here!)

Finding life's simple pleasures

At Dorset Cereals we love the simple pleasures of life, like a walk along a windswept beach or a great cup of tea in the garden at the end of the day. For us one of life's greatest simple pleasures is a proper breakfast. Perhaps that's because it provides a contemplative pause at the start of a busy day, or maybe it's the only meal when the whole family sits down to eat together.

We think breakfast is so important we wanted to make sure you have something to try for every occasion. We've divided the book into the following chapters:

Mood lifting ... easing you into the start of the day, breakfasts to give you back your mojo

Power breakfasts ... protein-packed energisers to help you cope with the demands of modern life – family, work, even finding time for you

Lazy Sundays ... the most heavenly breakfasts for cooking and eating in your pyjamas – while you read the papers

Big brunch ... breakfasts for sharing when you have a houseful and want something scrummy that everyone can dig into

Romantic mornings ... exquisite, filled-with-love breakfasts for just the two of you

Outdoors ... breakfast in the open air – no tricky ingredients and no awkward measures, food always tastes better outside

Takeaway ... pack a breakfast picnic and grab the early morning sun on the beach, in a field, on a hilltop; or breakfast on the way to work. Who said you had to eat at the table?

Comfort ... with a low effort-to-taste ratio, breakfasts that set you up for the day with a warm glow inside – the ultimate morning comfort foods

Breakfast isn't the only simple pleasure in life. Throughout the book we've sprinkled some of the other activities that make us feel great. From making the perfect pot of tea to leaping into the sea or building a camp fire, these are honest, natural and free activities and we've given you some tips to get you started. We relish doing them almost as much as we love making breakfast. Happy eating!

From all of us at Dorset Cereals
Poundbury, Dorset
dorsetcereals.co.uk

DORSET C.C.
ABBOTSBURY
WEYMOUTH
BUR
BRID

Studland Beach, Dorset

mood lifting

serves 2-3

warm grapefruit & orange *with* toasted coconut

An invigorating, caramelised, citrus fusion, mellowed with sweet toasted coconut – a great kickstart to your day.

- *2 large pink grapefruit*
- *3 navel oranges*
- *1 tbsp brown sugar*
- *15g / ½oz / 1 tbsp unsalted butter, cubed*
- *75g / 2½oz / 1 cup desiccated coconut*

Preheat the grill to high.

Using a sharp knife, cut the peel and membrane from the grapefruit and oranges, then slice the flesh into 1cm / ½in rings.

Arrange in a shallow baking dish. Sprinkle with the brown sugar and dot with the butter.

Grill until the fruit is lightly browned. Sprinkle with the coconut and return to the grill until just toasted.

Serve immediately.

serves 4

granola, *nectarine* & yoghurt *layer*

Enjoy your granola with a healthy twist. The creamy yoghurt and crunchy granola are a perfect counterfoil to the soft and juicy nectarines and raspberries. Mix it up by using your favourite flavoured yoghurt and seasonal fruits.

- *400ml / 14fl oz / 1¾ cups Greek yoghurt*
- *4 tbsp clear honey, plus extra for drizzling*
- *300g / 10½oz / 6 cups Dorset Cereals Honey Granola (or your choice)*
- *4 ripe nectarines, halved, stoned and sliced*
- *100g / 3½oz / ¾ cup raspberries*

Place the yoghurt in a bowl and mix with the honey.

Divide half the granola between 4 glasses, then add some of the nectarines and raspberries.

Follow with a layer of the yoghurt and honey mixture.

Repeat the layers, reserving some of the fruit for decorating on top, if desired. Finish with a drizzle of honey on top of each lovely glass.

serves 6

rhubarb & *clementine* bruschetta

A combination made in heaven! These two ingredients work their magic to bring a gentle start to your day.

- *400g / 14oz forced rhubarb, cut into 5cm / 2in lengths*
- *4 clementines, peeled and halved horizontally and segmented*
- *50g / 1¾oz / ¼ cup golden caster sugar*
- *12 x 1cm / ½in slices of baguette*

Preheat the oven to 200°C / 400°F / Gas Mark 6.

Place the rhubarb and clementines in a large, ovenproof dish and sprinkle over the golden caster sugar. Cover with foil and bake in the oven for 25 minutes until tender and juicy.

Lift off the foil, give the dish a shake and return to the oven for 5 minutes. Set aside to cool slightly.

Toast the baguette slices as you like them, place them on plates and pour over the rhubarb and clementine compote.

serves 6

cherry marys

The perfect hangover cure. It has just the right kick to get your mojo back after a night on the tiles.

For the cherry Marys

- *250g / 9oz cherry tomatoes*
- *200ml / 7fl oz / 7/8 cup vodka*
- *1 tbsp Worcestershire sauce*
- *1 tbsp sherry or balsamic vinegar*
- *a few drops of Tabasco sauce*
- *1 tsp celery salt*

For the dipping salt

- *1 tsp celery salt*
- *2 tbsp sea salt*
- *¼ tsp ground black pepper*

To make the cherry Marys

Score a cross in the base of each tomato with a sharp knife. Place in a sealable container cut side uppermost.

Whisk the vodka, Worcestershire sauce, sherry or balsamic vinegar, Tabasco, and celery salt. Pour gently over the tomatoes. Seal the container.

Place in the fridge for at least 2 hours or up to 2 days to allow the flavours to infuse.

Before serving, drain the tomatoes and arrange on a serving dish. (Reserve the leftover marinade to use for more cherry Marys or for a more traditional Bloody Mary.)

To make the dipping salt

Mix together the salts and pepper in a small dipping dish and place with the tomatoes.

serves 1

apple, *ginger* & mint *refresher*

We like to use green apples for this recipe because of the fabulous colour they give. Zingy and fresh, this drink is rocket fuel for the morning and beyond.

- *4 apples, cored and coarsely chopped*
- *2cm / ¾in ginger root, peeled and sliced*
- *6 sprigs fresh mint*
- *1 tbsp freshly squeezed lime juice*

Place half of the chopped apples in a blender and whiz until smooth – it may be necessary to add a little water depending on how juicy the apples are. Add the remaining ingredients and blend again until smooth.

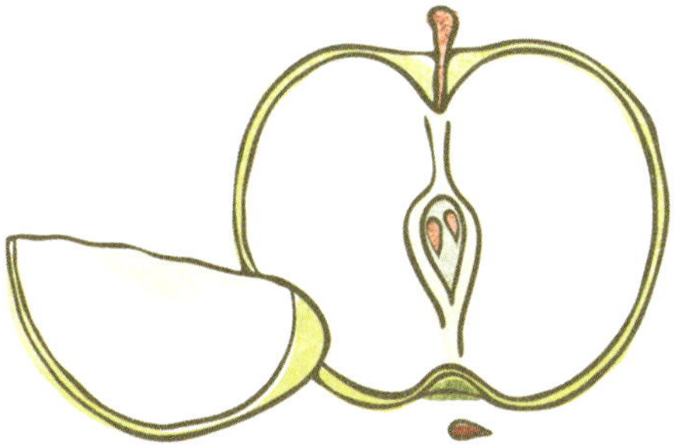

serves 4

vanilla *iced* coffee

If it's hot outside but you still need your coffee, look no further than this thirst-quencher. It will give you your caffeine fix and let you keep your cool.

- *4 heaped tbsp ground coffee*
- *250ml / 9fl oz / 1 1/8 cups whole milk*
- *5 tbsp soft brown sugar*
- *4 vanilla pods, split lengthways and deseeded (reserve the seeds)*
- *ice, to serve*

Pour 1 litre / 35fl oz of just-boiled water into a large jug and stir in the ground coffee. Cover and leave to infuse until cold.

Pour the milk into a small saucepan, then add the sugar and vanilla pods. Bring the milk to a simmer and remove from the heat. Leave for 25 minutes, then add the vanilla seeds and remove and reserve the vanilla pods.

When you are ready to serve, strain the coffee through a fine sieve and then through a coffee filter into a large, clean jug.

Put some ice in the bottom of four glasses; fill to within 2.5cm / 1in of the rim with the coffee and top with the vanilla milk.

Garnish with the vanilla pods and serve immediately.

serves 4

pineapple & mint *sparkling* refresher

Fruity and fresh – a sparkling way to get going first thing.

- *100g / 3½oz / ½ cup caster sugar*
- *600ml / 21fl oz / 2½ cups chilled sparkling water*
- *a small pineapple, peeled, cored and chopped*
- *a small handful of fresh mint*
- *ice, to serve*

Put the sugar and 100ml / 3½fl oz of the sparkling water into a saucepan over a low heat and stir occasionally until the sugar dissolves. Remove from the heat and cool.

Put the pineapple chunks in a blender with the cooled syrup and the mint, reserving 4 mint leaves to decorate. Blend until smooth.

Place a few ice cubes in 4 glasses, then divide the drink between the glasses, and top up with sparkling water. Garnish each with a reserved mint leaf and serve immediately.

simple #1 pleasure

wild swimming

Sea or lake, river or stream, there is no better simple pleasure than wild swimming – with not a sweaty changing room or smelly chlorine pool in sight.

The sheer delight of stepping into the cool, natural water of the sea or a local river gives a wonderful tingly feeling that sets your heart racing, and a sensation of being at one with nature – a rare thing in modern life. We know we sound like hippies, but if you haven't tried a wild swim, find your nearest spot (take a look at www.wildswimming.co.uk for ideas) and grab your opportunity. In Dorset, with the sea close by and an abundance of rivers, we are never very far from a wild swim. Whatever the weather, we see people off to play in nature's own swimming pools.

1. Wait for a hot day and prepare a breakfast picnic (see pages 138–157) to take down to the water's edge.

2. Jump in for a splash about – just about the best start to any day.

Isle of Purbeck, Dorset

3. Be sensible, though. Don't swim in rivers near where animals are grazing; if there's been a big storm; or close to industrial activity. Respect the wildlife and give swans a wide berth. If it's cold, invest in a wet suit. Oh, and generally keep your swimming kit on – or if you really feel like skinny dipping, make sure it's dark!

Studland Beach, Dorset

power breakfasts

makes 4

avocado & tomato *bruschetta*

A power-packed start to the day. Creamy avocado and tangy tomatoes are a perfect foil for each other in this recipe.

- *250g / 9oz / 1½ cups cherry tomatoes, halved*
- *4 tbsp extra virgin olive oil*
- *1 tbsp sherry vinegar or balsamic vinegar*
- *4 hand-cut slices good wholemeal bread*
- *1 avocado*
- *a handful of baby spinach leaves*
- *sea salt and ground black pepper*

Preheat the oven to 150°C / 300°F / Gas Mark 2.

Place the tomatoes in a non-stick oven dish and sprinkle with 1 tablespoon of the olive oil. Pop the dish into the oven and cook for up to 45 minutes until the tomatoes are caramelised (check frequently so they don't go too brown), then set aside.

Mix the vinegar with 2 tablespoons of olive oil and season with salt and pepper.

Toast the bread on a griddle pan and drizzle with the remaining olive oil.

Peel, stone and dice the avocado, then add to the tomatoes with the spinach. Divide the topping between the slices of toasted bread. Spoon the dressing over the top and serve.

serves 1

porridge – *with* granola & fresh fruit

A glorious combination of textures – soft and creamy porridge layered with crunchy granola and juicy fruit. How can you resist?

- *1 sachet Dorset Cereals Proper Porridge Oat & Barley*
- *160ml / 5¼fl oz / ⅔ cup whole milk*
- *sliced fresh fruit - nectarines, apricots, mango etc (whatever you fancy)*
- *30g / 1oz / ⅔ cup Dorset Cereals Honey Granola (or your choice)*

The easiest way to cook Proper Porridge, Oat & Barley is in the microwave. Or if you're feeling traditional, it's just as delicious made on the hob. Cooking porridge is a very personal thing. After all, it's an art, not a science.

Here's how we do it...

Newfangled way (microwave)
Pour the sachet of porridge and the milk (use slightly more or less, according to taste) into a deep microwavable bowl. Stir well, and cook on high for about 2–3 minutes (times vary by microwave type). Stir briskly and leave to stand for 1 minute.

Traditional way (on the hob)
Put the milk (according to taste) into a saucepan with the contents of the sachet of porridge and bring to the boil. Lower the heat and simmer for 2–3 minutes, stirring occasionally until the milk is absorbed and the porridge is creamy.

Place some of the sliced fruit in the bottom of the bowl, then half of the porridge topped with half of the granola. Repeat the layers, topping off with the remaining granola.

serves 4

ciabatta *– with* prosciutto *& poached* eggs

An Italian take on eggs Benedict, without the worry of making hollandaise sauce!

For the dressing

- *285ml / 10fl oz / 1¼ cups buttermilk*
- *1 tbsp Dijon mustard*
- *1 tbsp wholegrain mustard*
- *1-2 tbsp freshly squeezed lemon juice*
- *sea salt and ground black pepper*

For the poached eggs

- *4 large free-range eggs*
- *a good pinch of salt*
- *a drop of malt vinegar or white wine vinegar (optional)*
- *1 small ciabatta, halved horizontally*
- *100g / 3½oz prosciutto*

To make the dressing
Combine the buttermilk and mustards in a small bowl, stirring gently. Add the lemon juice and salt and pepper to taste.

To poach the eggs and assemble
Half-fill a medium saucepan with water and bring to the boil. Add the salt, and a drop of vinegar, if desired. Meanwhile, crack an egg into a small jug or bowl. Stir the boiling water vigorously with a balloon whisk until you have a whirlpool, then immediately slip the egg into the centre, lowering the jug 2cm / ¾in into the water. Turn the heat down low and cook for 3 minutes – use a timer to prevent overcooking.

Use a slotted spoon to scoop out the egg and then drain it on kitchen paper. Serve immediately. Repeat with the other eggs. If you're poaching in advance, drop each cooked egg straight into a bowl of iced water, or they will carry on cooking. To reheat, simply warm the eggs through in a pan of gently simmering water.

Meanwhile, lightly toast the ciabatta and cut each piece in half. Divide the prosciutto between the 4 pieces of ciabatta and top with the poached eggs. Gently drizzle the buttermilk dressing over the eggs and serve.

makes 12-16

peanut butter *energy bars*

Packed with protein-dense peanuts and ingredients to give you a real energy punch, these bars will carry you right through to lunchtime.

- *125g / 4½oz / 1 stick unsalted butter*
- *150g / 5½oz / ¾ cup soft brown sugar or light muscovado sugar*
- *125g / 4½oz / heaped ½ cup crunchy peanut butter (no added sugar variety)*
- *75g / 2½oz / 4½ tbsp clear honey, plus extra to finish*
- *finely grated zest of 1 orange*
- *finely grated zest of 1 unwaxed lemon*
- *150g / 5½oz / 1½ cups porridge oats (not jumbo)*
- *150g / 5½oz / 1½ cups muesli (such as Dorset Cereals Gloriously Nutty or Simply Nutty)*

Preheat the oven to 160°C / 325°F / Gas Mark 2–3.

Grease and line a baking tin, about 20cm / 8in square. Put the butter, sugar, peanut butter, honey and grated citrus zests in a deep saucepan over a very low heat. Leave until melted together, stirring from time to time. Remove from the heat.

Stir the oats and muesli into the melted butter mixture until thoroughly combined. Spread the mixture evenly into the baking tin, smoothing the top as you go.

Bake for about 30 minutes until golden in the centre and golden brown at the edges.

Leave to cool completely in the tin (it cuts much better when cold), then turn out and cut into squares. These bars will keep for 5–7 days in an airtight container.

For something different, replace the peanut butter with 1 medium-ripe banana. Mash the banana and stir it in after all the other ingredients have been combined.

serves 2

mango & cashew nut *smoothie*

Pure energy in a glass – and creamy and delicious too.

- *50g / 1¾oz / ½ cup cashew nuts, soaked overnight in cold water*
- *1 ripe mango, peeled, stoned and chopped*
- *1 tsp golden linseeds*

Drain the cashew nuts and place them in a blender with about 150ml / 5fl oz fresh water. Blend until smooth.

Add the mango and blend again until smooth.

Stir in the linseeds, pour into 2 glasses and serve immediately.

serves 4

strawberry *oatmeal* smoothie

We all know that oats are good for us and this is a lovely way to get your oats when you don't feel like porridge. You can use fresh or frozen berries. Peaches, apricots or nectarines are a lovely substitute, and for a winter twist, try the smoothie with plums.

- *100g / 3½oz / 1 cup porridge oats*
- *450ml / 16fl oz / 2 cups natural or flavoured yoghurt*
- *240ml / 8fl oz / 1 cup whole milk*
- *400g / 14oz strawberries, hulled and washed*
- *2 tbsp clear honey*

Place the porridge oats in a blender and process until they are finely ground – this step is essential so that your smoothie has a smooth texture.

Add the rest of the ingredients and process again until smooth.

We like this smoothie with a thick texture, but adjust with more milk if you prefer something a little more liquid.

simple #2 pleasure

skimming stones

A glassy lake, gentle river or calm sea gives the best results for skimming stones. The idea is to get your stone bouncing across the water: eight bounces is considered good, but the world record currently stands at 51!

1. Pick a thin, smooth and light stone and stand side on to the water.

2. Crouch down low, and launch your stone as fast as possible. You're aiming to get your stone moving low and horizontal over the surface of the water. Spinning the stone using a flick of the wrist will help it fly and reduce the air resistance.

3. Count the bounces and see if you can beat your friends and family.

Kimmeridge Bay, Dorset

lazy sundays

Puddletown, Dorset

serves 1

omelette – *with* gruyère & chives

The perfect omelette is one just tinged with gold on the surface and very soft and squidgy on the inside, so take care not to overcook.

- *2 or 3 large free-range eggs*
- *½ tsp Dijon mustard*
- *2 tbsp finely snipped fresh chives*
- *15g / ½oz / 1 tbsp unsalted butter*
- *25g / 1 oz / ¼ cup Gruyère, grated*
- *1 tbsp double cream*
- *sea salt and ground black pepper*

Whisk the eggs with some salt and pepper, the mustard and chives. Heat a frying pan over a high heat until it is hot. Add the butter and when it is sizzling, add the eggs. Let the eggs become golden on the outside, then draw the cooked edges into the middle so that the raw eggs can run to the edges. Continue until the omelette is almost set. This happens very quickly, about 30 seconds.

Remove from the heat and add the cheese and cream into the centre of the omelette. Fold the omelette over and slide on to a plate.

Season with salt and pepper to taste and garnish with some extra snipped chives, if desired. Serve immediately.

serves 5-6

mushroom stromboli

An all-in-one savoury bread – great for a Sunday picnic brunch. Make the dough and the filling the day before and just assemble in the morning; it is a lazy Sunday after all!

For the dough

- *450g / 1 lb / 3¼ cups strong white bread flour, plus extra for rolling*
- *2 tsp salt*
- *1 tsp dried yeast*
- *200ml / 7fl oz / ⅞ cup lukewarm water*

For the stromboli

- *1 tbsp olive oil*
- *15g / ½oz / 1 tbsp unsalted butter*
- *250g / 9oz / 3¾ cups chestnut, button or field mushrooms, sliced*
- *1 small onion, finely chopped*
- *2 garlic cloves, crushed*
- *100g / 3½oz / 2 cups baby leaf spinach*
- *100g / 3½oz / scant ½ cup cream cheese*
- *50g / 1¾oz Parmesan cheese, grated*
- *a handful of fresh parsley, chopped*
- *1 free-range egg, lightly beaten*
- *sea salt and ground black pepper*

To make the dough
Put the dry ingredients into a large mixing bowl and mix well. Make a well in the centre and add the lukewarm water. Combine with a wooden spoon. Cover and leave to rise for 2 hours, or leave in the refrigerator overnight.

To make the stromboli
Preheat the oven to 230°C / 450°F / Gas Mark 8.

Heat the olive oil and butter in a frying pan over a medium-low heat, then add the mushrooms, onion and garlic. Cook, stirring occasionally until most of the liquid has evaporated. Add the spinach and wilt into the mixture. Season well, with salt and pepper.

Flour your board, then knead the dough lightly and roll into a rectangle about 20cm x 30cm / 8in x 12in. Spread the cream cheese lengthways down the dough and spread the mushroom mixture on top. Sprinkle with the Parmesan and parsley.

Bring the long edges of the dough together and press to seal, then press the short edges to seal. You should have a long roll.

Place the roll on to a floured baking tray, seam side down. Brush with the beaten egg. Make a few shallow slashes along the roll to allow steam to escape. Bake for 25–30 minutes until golden brown. Serve in slices.

serves 4

rosti — *with* crispy bacon

Crunchy golden potato on the outside, soft and creamy on the inside – these rosti make an irresistible breakfast teamed with some crispy bacon. Cooking the bacon in the oven is easy and you don't have to worry about fitting all the bacon into one pan at the same time.

- *2 medium-sized waxy potatoes*
- *8 rashers of streaky bacon*
- *15g / ½oz / 1 tbsp unsalted butter*
- *1 tbsp goose fat*
- *sea salt and ground black pepper*

Parboil the potatoes in salted water until just tender but not soft. Allow to cool and chill for at least 2 hours.

Preheat the oven to 200°C /400°F/ Gas Mark 6.

Place a wire rack on to a baking tray and arrange the bacon in one layer on the rack.

Bake the rashers in the oven for 15–20 minutes until they are as crispy as you like them. Drain them on paper towels.

Coarsely grate the potatoes and season with salt and pepper. Heat half the butter and half the goose fat in a small, heavy-based frying pan until sizzling, then add the grated potato. Cook for a couple of minutes before pressing lightly into a flat cake.

Cook the potato cake for 2 minutes, and then gently shake the pan to loosen. Continue to cook for about 10 minutes until golden and crisp. Place a plate on top of the pan and invert both together so that the rosti is cooked side uppermost on the plate.

Add the rest of the butter and goose fat to the pan and when sizzling, slide the rosti back into the pan cooked side uppermost. Cook for another 10 minutes, or until golden.

Serve the rosti cut into wedges with the crispy bacon rashers.

serves 2

scrambled eggs — *with* smoked trout

A great, easy dish for when you are feeling a bit lazy. The recipe is easily scaled up if you need to make more. If you overcook your eggs a little they can be rescued by stirring in a tablespoon or two of mayonnaise.

- *2 smoked trout fillets*
- *4 large free-range eggs*
- *120ml / 4fl oz / ½ cup single cream*
- *a knob of unsalted butter*
- *sea salt and ground black pepper*

Put each smoked trout fillet on a plate and set aside.

Put the eggs and cream in a bowl and season with salt and pepper. Lightly whisk until all the ingredients are just combined.

Heat a non-stick frying pan over a low heat for 1 minute, then add the butter and let it melt (don't allow the butter to brown or it will discolour the eggs). Pour in the egg mixture and let it sit without stirring for 20 seconds.

Stir with a wooden spoon, lifting and folding it over from the bottom of the pan. Let it sit for another 10 seconds, then stir and fold again, being careful not to over-stir.

Repeat until the eggs are softly set and slightly runny in places, then remove from the heat and leave for a few seconds to finish cooking.

Give the eggs a final stir and serve straightaway with the smoked trout.

serves 2

mackerel — *with* pink grapefruit & fennel

The sharpness from the pink grapefruit beautifully offsets the oiliness from the mackerel, while the slightly aniseedy fennel provides some crisp texture. This is lovely eaten in the garden on a glorious summer's day.

- *4 mackerel fillets*
- *2 tbsp olive oil, plus extra for cooking*
- *1 pink grapefruit, peeled and segmented; juice reserved*
- *½ fennel bulb, sliced, and feathery fronds, chopped and reserved*
- *sea salt and ground black pepper*

Preheat the grill to high. Brush the mackerel with a little oil, season with salt and pepper, and grill for 8 minutes, or until the skin is translucent and the flesh is flaking. Mix the grapefruit juice with the oil. Stir through the fennel and grapefruit segments and add the chopped fennel fronds. Season again and scatter over the mackerel fillets.

serves 6

roasted tomato & pancetta *clafoutis*

Another delicious Sunday breakfast option, best served with some crusty bread or a simple leaf salad. Put the whole lot in the middle of the table and let everyone dig in.

- *500g / 1lb 2oz cherry tomatoes*
- *2 tbsp olive oil*
- *1 tbsp chopped fresh thyme*
- *2 garlic cloves, crushed*
- *2 tsp caster sugar*
- *200g / 7oz pancetta slices*
- *250ml / 9fl oz / 1⅛ cups single cream*
- *3 large free-range eggs*
- *2 tbsp plain flour*
- *250g / 9oz mozzarella cheese, grated*
- *sea salt and ground black pepper*

Preheat the oven to 200°C / 400°F / Gas Mark 6.

Arrange the tomatoes in a single layer in a shallow baking dish. Drizzle with the oil, then sprinkle with the thyme, garlic and sugar, and salt and pepper to taste. Roast in the oven for 10–15 minutes, or until the skin shrivels slightly.

Meanwhile, place the pancetta on a baking tray and cook in the oven for 12 minutes, allow to cool and then break into small pieces. Sprinkle the pancetta pieces over the tomatoes.

In a blender, blitz the cream, eggs and flour until smooth; pour over the tomatoes.

Sprinkle with the mozzarella. Reduce the temperature to 180°C / 350°F / Gas Mark 4 and bake for about 25 minutes, or until puffed and golden. Serve immediately.

serves 4

danish *puff* pancakes *(Æbleskivers)*

A lazy Sunday is the best time to potter in the kitchen and try something new. Pancake meets doughnut in these Danish puffs. Once you've mastered the technique, add a little lemon curd or Nutella halfway through cooking. Yum! Traditionally, you'd use a knitting needle to turn them.

- *175g / 6oz / 1⅓ cups plain flour*
- *2½ tsp baking powder*
- *¼ tsp salt*
- *3 tbsp caster sugar*
- *1 large free-range egg*
- *225ml / 7¾fl oz / 1 cup whole milk*
- *30g / 1oz / 2 tbsp unsalted butter, melted, plus extra for brushing*
- *icing sugar, for dusting*
- *homemade jam (page 178), to serve*

Sift the flour, baking powder and salt into a bowl, add the sugar and thoroughly combine. Beat the egg with the milk and butter. Add the wet ingredients to the dry ingredients and stir until evenly mixed.

Place an æbleskiver pan over a medium-low heat. When the pan is hot enough to make a drop of water dance, brush the cups with additional melted butter and fill each to slightly below the rim with the batter.

After about 1½ minutes a thin crust will have formed on the bottom of the cups. Pierce the crust with a thin wooden skewer, or cocktail stick, and gently pull the shell to rotate the pancake balls until about half of the cooked crust is above the rim and the batter flows into the cup.

Cook for about another minute until the crust is firm, then rotate the ball again until the top is covered by all-cooked pancake. Continue to cook, turning occasionally until the balls are evenly browned and no longer moist in the centre, about 10–12 minutes.

Check by piercing the last pancake ball with the skewer, it should come out clean. Repeat with remaining batter; keep the pancakes balls warm in a napkin-lined basket.

Dust with icing sugar and serve with a spoonful of homemade jam.

serves 4

oven pancakes *– with* berries

No need to panic about flipping pancakes with this recipe! It's also easy to adapt it to serve more people. The best bit is that there's no need to worry about timing: the pancakes are all made in the oven at the same time. Delicious served with lemon curd, chocolate spread or homemade jam (page 178).

- *100g / 3½oz / ¾ cup raspberries, halved*
- *100g / 3½oz / ¾ cup blueberries, halved*
- *100g / 3½oz / ¾ cup strawberries, sliced*
- *1 tbsp caster sugar*
- *30g / 1oz / 2 tbsp unsalted butter, melted, plus 4 tsp for the dishes*
- *3 large free-range eggs*
- *125ml / 4fl oz / ½ cup whole milk*
- *70g / 2½oz / heaped ½ cup plain flour*
- *1 tsp good vanilla extract*
- *1 tsp grated orange zest*
- *¾ tsp salt*
- *icing sugar, for dusting*

Preheat the oven to 220°C / 425°F / Gas Mark 7.

Gently combine the berries and sugar in a small bowl and set aside while you make the pancakes.

Place 4 individual ovenproof dishes (15cm x 15cm / 6in x 6in) on to a baking tray and add 1 teaspoon of butter to each dish.

Whisk the eggs, then add the milk and keep whisking. Slowly add the flour, vanilla, orange zest, the melted butter, and the salt. Mix until smooth.

Place the dishes in the oven for 1 minute until the butter is hot and bubbly, ensuring the butter covers the bottom of each dish. Immediately divide the batter between the dishes and bake for 12–14 minutes until puffy and lightly brown.

Turn out the pancakes onto a serving plate. Divide the berries among them, dust with icing sugar and serve hot.

serves 6

strawberry *breakfast* risotto

Breakfast in the garden – what more perfect way to spend it than with a light and gorgeous strawberry risotto? If you're feeling decadent, treat yourself to some pink bubbly to go with it!

- *50g / 1¾oz / 3½ tbsp unsalted butter*
- *200g / 7oz / 1⅛ cups arborio rice*
- *240ml / 8fl oz / 1 cup single cream*
- *100g / 3½oz / ½ cup caster sugar*
- *2 tsp good vanilla extract*
- *200g / 7oz / 1½ cups strawberries, sliced*

In a large saucepan bring 1 litre / 35fl oz water to a simmer over a medium heat, then reduce the heat to low. You'll need this hot water to make the risotto.

Place another large pan over a medium heat and add the butter. When it has melted, add the rice and stir until it is all coated.

Add the cream, sugar and vanilla and cook for 1 minute, stirring gently. Increase the heat to medium-high and stir in one ladle of the hot water, then stir frequently until the water is absorbed.

Continue stirring and adding a ladle of hot water at a time, allowing each ladle to be absorbed before adding the next.

Cook until the rice is tender and the risotto has a creamy consistency, about 25 minutes.

Remove from the heat and stir in the strawberries until the risotto is light pink.

Serve while still warm.

simple pleasure #3

the perfect cup of tea

Few things are as good with breakfast as a perfectly brewed cup of tea.

1. Always use high-quality loose leaf tea, and store it in an air-tight container at room temperature. Use 1 rounded teaspoon for each cup you intend to serve.

2. Use freshly drawn water – that way it will contain lots of oxygen to give your tea the best flavour.

3. Put the tea in a warm pot, add freshly boiled water, brew for 3–4 minutes, then serve. Ahhh, that's better.

Wimborne, Dorset

big brunch

savoury bread *&* butter pudding *– with maple-glazed* bacon

serves 4-6

Breakfast for the masses made easy. A little light onion cooking, some assembling and then pop it all in the oven. What could be simpler? Leave out the bacon if you're serving vegetarians.

- *30g / 1oz / 2 tbsp unsalted butter*
- *1 onion, finely chopped*
- *2 tbsp finely chopped fresh parsely*
- *1 tbsp snipped fresh chives*
- *6 large free-range eggs*
- *750ml / 26fl oz / 3¼ cups whole milk*
- *200g / 7oz day-old good bread or brioche, cut into 2cm / ¾in cubes*
- *125g / 4½oz Cheddar cheese, grated*
- *12 rashers of dry-cured streaky bacon*
- *2 tbsp good maple syrup*
- *sea salt and ground black pepper*

Melt the butter in a frying pan over a medium-high heat. Add the onion and cook until softened but not browned, stirring occasionally. Remove from the heat and stir in the parsley and chives.

In a large bowl, whisk the eggs with the milk and season with salt and pepper.

Butter a 3-litre / 105fl oz / 3 quart baking dish. Place half of the bread cubes in the dish and sprinkle with half of the onion and Cheddar, then repeat the layers. Gently pour over the milk mixture and leave it to rest for 30–60 minutes.

Preheat the oven to 190°C / 375°F / Gas Mark 5. Bake the pudding in the middle of the oven for 45 minutes until puffed and golden.

Lay the bacon on a wire rack over a baking tray and drizzle with the maple syrup. Pop the baking tray into the oven 20 minutes before the pudding will finish baking.

Serve the pudding alongside the bacon – enjoy.

serves 4

gingerbread oat *pancakes*

A great way to spice up your pancakes! For a fun twist, you could use your cookie cutters to make gingerbread-men shapes.

- *75g / 2½oz / heaped ½ cup plain flour*
- *2 sachets Dorset Cereals Gingerbread Porridge*
- *1 tsp baking powder*
- *½ tsp bicarbonate of soda*
- *½ tsp sea salt*
- *170ml / 5½fl oz / ⅔ cup buttermilk or natural yoghurt*
- *2 tbsp sunflower oil, plus extra for frying*
- *1 large free-range egg*
- *clear honey or golden syrup, to serve (optional)*
- *slices of ripe pear, to serve (optional)*

Put the flour, Gingerbread Porridge, baking powder, bicarbonate of soda, salt, buttermilk or natural yoghurt, oil and egg in a food processor or blender and blitz until smooth.

Heat a lightly oiled frying pan over a medium-high heat. Pour or ladle a quarter of the batter into the pan. Cook until you see bubbles appearing on the top of the pancake. Turn over and cook for about a minute until golden. Repeat for the remaining batter.

Delicious served with a drizzle of honey or golden syrup and some slices of fresh pear.

makes 12

classic fruit, nut *and* seed muffins

Prepare this simple mixture the night before you want to eat the muffins and simply bake in the morning. You will be the host with the most!

- *250g / 9oz / heaped 1¾ cups plain flour*
- *2½ tsp baking powder*
- *½ tsp bicarbonate of soda*
- *100g / 3½oz /½ cup caster sugar*
- *1 tsp ground ginger*
- *¼ tsp mixed spice*
- *2 unwaxed lemons*
- *approx 125ml / 4fl oz / ½ cup whole milk or natural yoghurt*
- *75g / 2½oz / 5 tbsp unsalted butter, melted and left to cool*
- *1 large free-range egg*
- *100g / 3½oz/ 1 cup Dorset Cereals Classic Fruits, Roasted Nuts & Seeds*
- *1 tbsp demerara sugar*

Sieve the flour, baking powder, bicarbonate of soda, sugar, ginger and mixed spice into a large bowl, then cover with a clean tea towel and leave overnight.

In the morning, preheat the oven to 200°C / 400°F / Gas Mark 6. Place 12 muffin cases in a a muffin tin.

Grate the zest of the lemons over the dry ingredients.

Juice the lemons and add milk or yoghurt until the volume comes up to 200ml / 7fl oz. Add the cooled melted butter and the egg. Whisk lightly. Pour the wet ingredients into the dry ingredients and stir until just combined. Fold in the muesli.

Divide the mixture between the 12 muffin cases and sprinkle with the demerara sugar. Bake for 20 minutes, or until golden brown.

serves 6

kedgeree – *with* smoked mackerel

We have loads of mackerel in Dorset and lots of great smokeries, so this is a favourite. Mackerel not only tastes great and is plentiful, but it's also really good for you.

- *40g / 1½oz / 3 tbsp unsalted butter*
- *1 tbsp olive oil*
- *1 onion, finely chopped*
- *250g / 9oz / 1¼ cups basmati rice*
- *2 tsp dried coriander*
- *1 tsp dried cumin*
- *4 cardamom pods, crushed*
- *1 tsp dried turmeric*
- *1 cinnamon stick, broken*
- *600ml / 21fl oz / 2½ cups vegetable stock*
- *450g / 1lb smoked mackerel*
- *3 large free-range eggs*
- *3 large spring onions, finely sliced*
- *sea salt and ground black pepper*

Melt the butter with the oil in a large saucepan. Add the onion and fry lightly for 5 minutes until it softens.

Add the rice and spices and stir to coat with the oil and butter. When everything is coated, add the stock and bring to the boil, then cover with a lid and simmer for 10–12 minutes.

Skin the mackerel and flake into large pieces. Add the fish to the rice pan, season and give a gentle stir. Cover again and leave off the heat for 10 minutes.

Hard boil the eggs for 8 minutes. When they are cool enough to handle, peel them and cut them into quarters.

Fluff up the rice before serving, then garnish with the eggs and sliced spring onions.

serves 6

sweetcorn fritters – *with* tomato *salsa*

These colourful fritters are very moreish and perfect for a big family brunch.

For the fritters

- *500g / 1lb 2oz / 3½ cups cooked corn kernels, from cobs or frozen*
- *2 large free-range eggs*
- *125g / 4½oz / 1 cup plain flour*
- *1 tsp baking powder*
- *2 spring onions, finely sliced*
- *unsalted butter, for greasing*
- *sea salt and ground white pepper*

For the tomato salsa

- *3 large plum tomatoes, cubed*
- *1–2 red chillies, deseeded and finely sliced*
- *2 spring onions, finely sliced*
- *1 small handful of fresh flat-leaf parsley, finely chopped*
- *1 tsp freshly squeezed lemon juice*
- *1 tbsp extra virgin olive oil*
- *sea salt and ground black pepper*

To make the fritters
Preheat the oven to 120°C / 250°F / Gas Mark ½.

Place half the corn with the eggs, flour and baking powder in a blender. Season with salt and pepper, then whizz until smooth. Fold in the remaining corn and the spring onions.

Heat a frying pan over a medium-high heat and lightly grease with butter. For each fritter drop 1–2 tablespoons of batter into the pan and cook for about a minute on each side until golden. Drain on kitchen paper and keep warm in the oven while you cook the rest.

To make the tomato salsa
Mix all the ingredients together gently, then season with salt and pepper to taste. Serve with the sweetcorn fritters and all garnished with extra parsley.

serves 8

cheese & herb *share bread*

A real crowd-pleaser, this is great for feeding the hungry hordes after a sleepover.

- *1 unsliced rustic white loaf*
- *250g / 9oz Cheddar cheese, grated*
- *4 spring onions, finely sliced*
- *2 generous handfuls of fresh herbs, chopped (flat-leaf parsley, chives, oregano)*
- *60g / 2oz / 4 tbsp unsalted butter, melted*

Preheat the oven to 180°C / 350°F / Gas Mark 4.

Slice the bread almost all the way through in a cross-hatch pattern, leaving 2cm / ¾in between the slices.

Place the grated cheese in a large bowl, mix in the spring onions and herbs, then gently stir in the melted butter.

Lay the bread on a large sheet of tinfoil on a baking tray. Stuff the cheese mixture between the slices, then wrap the bread in the tinfoil. (At this point you can refrigerate the bread until you are ready to bake.)

Pop the bread into the oven and bake for 15 minutes, then unwrap the loaf from the foil and bake for another 10 minutes until the cheese has melted.

Place on a board to serve.

serves 4-6

cheese & ham quesadillas

These are fun and so easy to make. Follow the recipe as detailed below, or go free-style with your own fillings – either savoury or sweet.

- *8 small tortillas or flatbreads*
- *200g / 7oz Cheddar cheese, grated*
- *8 slices good ready-to-eat ham*
- *4 spring onions, finely sliced*

Arrange 4 tortillas or flatbreads on a clean worktop. Sprinkle half the cheese and spring onions over the tortillas and then lay the ham slices on top, using two slices per tortilla. Cover with the rest of the cheese and spring onions and top with the remaining tortillas.

Heat a frying pan over a medium heat. Place one quesadilla in the pan and cook for about 3 minutes on each side. Remove from the pan and keep warm while you are cooking the rest. Cut into wedges and serve immediately.

serves 6–8

baked egg baguettes

Cheesy eggs, light and fluffy, baked in a bread crust – like a little hand-held soufflé.

- *100g / 3½oz pancetta, finely chopped*
- *4 small wholemeal baguettes*
- *5 large free-range eggs*
- *85ml / 2¾fl oz / ⅓ cup double cream*
- *75g / 2½oz Gruyère cheese, grated*
- *2 spring onions, finely sliced*
- *sea salt and ground black pepper*

Preheat the oven to 180°C / 350F° / Gas Mark 4.

Lightly grease a frying pan and fry the pancetta over a medium-high heat until crisp. Set aside.

Cut a deep 'V' lengthways through the tops of each baguette until about 1cm / ½in from the bottom. Open them out and remove some of the bread.

Place the eggs and cream into a mixing bowl and lightly beat together. Whisk in the remaining ingredients including the crisped pancetta and a light seasoning of salt and pepper.

Pour equal amounts of the mixture into each baguette and place on a baking tray.

Bake for 20–25 minutes, or until golden brown, puffed and set in the centre. Allow to cool for about 5 minutes, then cut and serve.

serves 6

cheese & bacon popcorn

When you have a crowd for breakfast serve them this fun and tasty snack. It will give them something to talk about – who else would make them cheese and bacon popcorn? Prepare the bacon and cheese the night before and it will take only minutes to put this together in the morning.

- *50g / 1¾ oz Parmesan cheese, grated*
- *3 tbsp pine nuts*
- *3 rashers of back or streaky bacon*
- *1 tbsp snipped fresh chives*
- *a pinch of sea salt*
- *5 tbsp extra virgin olive oil*
- *100g / 3½oz / 4 quarts popped popcorn (made from ½ cup unpopped)*

Preheat the oven to 160°C / 325°F / Gas Mark 2–3.

Spread out the Parmesan on a lined baking tray, bake for 7 minutes, remove from the oven and leave to cool.

Heat a frying pan over a medium heat and dry fry the pine nuts, shaking occasionally until golden and toasted. Set aside. Lightly grease the same frying pan and fry the bacon rashers over a medium-high heat until crisp. When the bacon is cool enough to handle, crumble it into a bowl and set aside.

Whizz the Parmesan, bacon, pine nuts, chives and salt, together with 2 tablespoons of olive oil in a food processor.

Place the popcorn on to a baking tray and warm in the oven for 5 minutes.

Meanwhile, heat the remaining oil in a small saucepan until warm.

Remove the popcorn from the oven; pour over the warm olive oil, followed by the cheese and bacon and stir lightly to coat.

Serve either in a large bowl or small individual bowls.

serves 4

pea pancakes – *with smoked salmon* & crème fraîche

An easy and colourful twist on that breakfast classic – pancakes. Treat them with care to maintain an emerald-green appearance. A beautiful plate, served with lovely pink smoked salmon.

- *200g / 7oz / 1⅓ cups fresh or frozen peas*
- *1 large free-range egg*
- *2 tbsp plain flour*
- *2 tbsp sunflower oil*
- *200g / 7oz smoked salmon*
- *1 lemon*
- *1 small pot crème fraîche*
- *sea salt and ground black pepper*

Blanch the peas for 1–2 minutes in a pan of boiling water until tender, drain and then cool under running cold water. Reserve about a third of the peas until later.

Purée the rest of the peas in a blender with the egg until smooth; add a tablespoon of water if necessary.

Decant the pea purée to a bowl and whisk in the flour. Season with salt and pepper and stir in the reserved peas. The result should be the consistency of pancake batter – adjust with water or flour, if necessary.

Place 1 tablespoon of oil into a frying pan and place over a medium-high heat. Spoon the batter into the pan to make pancake shapes, each 1cm / ½in thick, being careful not to overcrowd the pan. Cook gently for about 3 minutes on each side, making sure not to colour the pancakes too much.

Remove the pancakes when cooked and keep warm. Repeat with the remaining batter, using another tablespoon of oil if necessary.

Top the warm pancakes with smoked salmon and a squeeze of lemon juice, and season with pepper. Serve immediately with a dollop of crème fraîche.

serves 4

bubble & squeak – with honey & mustard sausages

A much-loved classic, this is a wonderful and filling breakfast that will set you up for the day ahead.

- 1 tbsp olive oil
- 8 good pork sausages
- 2 tbsp Dijon mustard
- 2 tbsp clear honey
- 300g / 10½oz / 1½ cups boiled potatoes
- 200g / 7oz / 3 cups cooked greens (cabbage, kale, brussels sprouts etc)
- a knob of butter
- sea salt and ground black pepper

Preheat the oven to 180°C / 350°F / Gas Mark 4.

In an ovenproof frying pan, heat the oil over a medium-high heat. Add the sausages and cook for 7–8 minutes, turning occasionally until browned.

In a small bowl, mix the mustard and honey together. Brush the sausages with the honey and mustard mixture and place the pan in the oven. Bake the sausages for about 15 minutes, turning twice and basting with the juices.

Take your boiled spuds out of the fridge an hour in advance, then mash them with a fork. Finely shred your cooked greens and mix them in with the potato and salt and pepper to taste. Melt a knob of butter in a non-stick frying pan and, when it sizzles, add the potato mixture. Press down and smooth flat, then leave to fry over a moderate heat until a thin crust has formed.

Turn over to cook both sides, then serve in wedges with the sausages.

serves 4

french *toast* sandwich

A bit naughty but absolutely delicious and really quick to make. If you feel like it, you could add sliced strawberries or blueberries to the filling, or even some crispy bacon, maple syrup or lemon curd.

- *125g / 4½oz/ ½ cup mascarpone*
- *1 tbsp caster sugar*
- *1 tsp freshly squeezed lemon juice*
- *1 tsp good vanilla extract*
- *8 slices good white bread or brioche*
- *2 large free-range eggs*
- *125ml / 4fl oz / ½ cup whole milk*
- *a pinch of salt*
- *15g / ½oz / 1 tbsp unsalted butter*

In a bowl whisk the mascarpone, sugar, lemon juice and ½ teaspoon of the vanilla extract together. Divide between 4 of the bread or brioche slices, leaving a 6mm / ¼in border on all sides. Top with the remaining bread slices.

Make the batter by whisking the eggs, milk, remaining vanilla extract and salt together. Pour into a baking dish.

Place each of the sandwiches in the batter and allow to stand for 5 seconds, turn and repeat.

Meanwhile, melt half the butter in a frying pan over a medium-high heat. Carefully lift the sandwiches from the batter using a large spatula and transfer to the frying pan. Cook for 3 minutes, then add the rest of the butter, turn the sandwiches and cook for a further 2–3 minutes until golden.

Remove the sandwiches to a chopping board. Cut each sandwich diagonally and serve.

serves 2

spring eggs – with peas, beans & mushrooms

A lovely fresh start to the day. Gently cooked peas and beans with softly set eggs are crowned with scented basil oil – heaven!

- a small handful of fresh basil leaves
- 4 tbsp olive oil
- 30g / 1oz / 2 tbsp unsalted butter
- a handful chestnut mushrooms
- 1 shallot, finely chopped
- 100g / 3½oz / ⅔ cup fresh or frozen peas, blanched
- 100g / 3½oz / ⅞ cup fresh or frozen broad beans, blanched
- 4 large free-range eggs
- 2 tbsp crème fraîche
- 4 or 5 sundried tomatoes, sliced
- sea salt and ground black pepper

Bring a small pot of water to the boil and blanch the basil leaves for 15 seconds. Drain and cool in cold running water. Squeeze out the excess water. Place the leaves in a blender, season with salt and pepper and blend while adding the olive oil until you have a smooth purée. Add a few tablespoons of water, if necessary.

Heat a frying pan over a medium-high heat and melt the butter. Add the mushrooms and sauté until tender. Add the shallot and cook for another 2 minutes, then season with salt and pepper. Add the peas and broad beans and sauté for 1 minute. Break each egg into a bowl and then add it to the pan. Cook until set, about 2 minutes. Drizzle over a few spoonfuls of basil purée and the crème fraîche, and sprinkle over the slices of sundried tomato. Season with salt and pepper. Serve in bowls immediately, with crusty bread to mop up the juices.

serves 4

breakfast tart

A twist on the classic bacon and eggs, this tart has none of the last-minute timing issues you might have when cooking a full English for a hungry gathering.

- *1 x 500g / 1lb 2oz block ready-to-roll puff pastry*
- *4 large free-range eggs, plus 1 extra lightly beaten for glazing*
- *8 rashers of streaky bacon*
- *75g / 2½oz / ⅓ cup crème fraîche*
- *50g / 1¾oz Gruyère cheese, grated*
- *a few fresh chives, snipped, to decorate*
- *sea salt and ground black pepper*

Preheat the oven to 220°C / 425°F / Gas Mark 7. Lightly grease a baking tray.

On a lightly floured surface, roll out the puff pastry to ½cm / ¼in thick and cut into a 30cm x 20cm / 12in x 8in rectangle. Place the pastry on the prepared baking tray. Using a paring knife, score a border 1cm / ½in from the edge of the pastry. Using a fork, prick the centre of the pastry. Brush the border with the beaten egg and refrigerate for 15 minutes.

Lightly grease a frying pan and fry the bacon over a medium-high heat until crisp. Set aside.

In a small bowl, stir together the crème fraîche and cheese, and season with salt and pepper. Spread the crème fraîche mixture on to the pastry, keeping the border clean. Lay the bacon on top, slightly overlapping the slices.

Bake the tart for 15 minutes, rotating the baking tray halfway through baking.

Remove the baking tray from the oven and place it on a level heatproof surface. Using a fork, prick any large air pockets in the pastry. Crack the eggs on to the tart, spacing them 5cm / 2in apart. Return to the oven and bake until the egg whites are set and the yolks still soft, about 7–10 minutes.

Transfer the tart to a platter, decorate with the chives, and serve immediately.

serves 10

granola

Dorset Cereals makes great granolas (well, we would say that, wouldn't we?), but if you really want to have a go...

- *2 tbsp sunflower oil*
- *100ml / 3½fl oz / scant ½ cup maple syrup*
- *4 tbsp clear honey*
- *1 tbsp good vanilla extract*
- *300g / 10½oz / heaped 3 cups rolled oats*
- *25g / 1oz / 3 tbsp sunflower seeds*
- *50g / 1¾oz / 6 tbsp pumpkin seeds*
- *100g / 3½oz / ⅞ cup flaked or chopped nuts*
- *50g / 1¾oz / ¾ cup flaked or desiccated coconut*
- *100g / 3½oz / ⅔ cup dried fruit (cranberries, apricots, blueberries, raisins, etc)*
- *natural yoghurt and fresh fruit, to serve (optional)*

Preheat the oven to 150°C / 300°F / Gas Mark 2.

Mix the oil, maple syrup, honey and vanilla in a bowl. Add the dry ingredients except for the dried fruit and coconut, and mix well.

Spread the mixture over two baking trays and bake in the oven for 15 minutes, then add the coconut and mix. Bake for another 10–15 minutes.

Remove from the oven and turn out on to another baking tray to cool. When cool, add the dried fruit and stir to mix.

The granola will keep in an airtight container for two weeks.

Delicious served with yoghurt and fresh fruit, if desired.

serves 6

huevos rancheros

A classic breakfast dish from Mexico. We like to serve the salsa, beans and crème fraîche separately, so that everyone can make their huevos rancheros as they like them.

For the salsa

- *6 tomatoes, deseeded and cubed*
- *4 spring onions, finely sliced*
- *finely grated zest and juice of 1 lime*
- *1 green chilli, finely diced*
- *a handful of fresh coriander, chopped (optional)*

For the tortillas

- *1 tsp olive oil*
- *6 corn or wheat tortillas*
- *100g / 3½oz Cheddar cheese, grated*
- *6 large free-range eggs*
- *1 x 400g / 14oz can black beans, drained and rinsed*
- *a small pot of crème fraîche*
- *sea salt and ground black pepper*

To make the salsa

Mix together the cubed tomatoes, spring onions, and zest and juice of the lime to taste.

Add the chilli – leave the seeds in if you like it hot, take them out if you don't! Add the coriander (if using), season with salt and pepper, give it a stir and set aside until you are ready to serve.

To make the tortillas

Oil a heavy-based frying pan and place over a medium heat. Add a tortilla and cook until lightly golden on the bottom. Flip the tortilla over and sprinkle with cheese.

Crack an egg on to the cheese and season with salt and pepper (don't worry if it looks messy). Continue to cook until the egg white is about halfway cooked and the yolk is still runny. Carefully flip the tortilla over and cook for another minute or two. Flip the tortilla on to a plate. Repeat for the other tortillas.

Serve the tortillas with the salsa, black beans and crème fraîche.

serves 2–3

chorizo & onion *tortilla*

A sweet and spicy taste of the Mediterranean. Make this tortilla the night before you want to eat it, and then enjoy it either at room temperature or warm.

- *4 tbsp olive oil*
- *100g / 3½oz / ¾ cup good cooking chorizo, skin removed*
- *3 medium potatoes, peeled and thinly sliced*
- *1 onion, halved lengthways and finely sliced*
- *5 large free-range eggs*
- *sea salt and ground black pepper*

Heat 1 tablespoon of the oil in a frying pan, and add the chorizo. Break up the meat with a wooden spoon as it is cooking. Cook over a medium heat until slightly golden, about 8 minutes. Remove from the pan and drain on kitchen paper.

Wipe out the frying pan, add 2 tablespoons of oil and place over a medium-low heat. Layer the potatoes and onion in the pan, seasoning as you go. Cook for 10–15 minutes, turning the ingredients over occasionally. Do not allow the potatoes and onion to brown too much.

Meanwhile, beat the eggs in a large bowl. When the potatoes and onion are cooked, remove with a slotted spoon and add to the eggs with the chorizo meat. Stir gently to coat all the ingredients.

Return to the pan, adding the remaining oil if necessary, and spreading the mixture evenly. Cook over a medium-low heat until the base is golden brown and the top is almost set.

Place a plate over the pan and invert the tortilla and slide back into the pan with the golden brown side uppermost. Cook for 2–3 minutes more.

This tortilla is delicious served hot or at room temperature.

toasted coconut & spelt bread *— with* berry compote

serves 6

One for sharing: serve a pile of toasted slices of the loaf alongside a big bowl of tangy berry compote – and dive in.

For the coconut bread

- *300g / 10½oz / 2¼ cups plain flour*
- *2 tsp baking powder*
- *2 tsp ground cinnamon*
- *225g / 8oz / 1 ⅛ cups caster sugar*
- *150g / 5½oz / 2 cups desiccated coconut*
- *75g / 2½oz / ¾ cup Dorset Cereals Tasty Toasted Spelt Flakes*
- *2 large free-range eggs*
- *300ml / 10½fl oz / 1¼ cups whole milk*
- *1 tsp good vanilla extract*
- *75g / 2½oz / 5 tbsp unsalted butter, melted*
- *icing sugar, to serve (optional)*

For the berry compote

- *a knob of unsalted butter*
- *2 tsp caster sugar*
- *1 tsp good vanilla extract*
- *400g / 14oz mixed berries*

To make the coconut bread

Preheat the oven to 180°C / 350°F / Gas Mark 4. Grease and flour a 21cm x 10cm / 8¼in x 4in loaf tin.

Sift the flour, baking powder and cinnamon into a mixing bowl. Add the sugar, coconut and muesli and stir to mix.

Lightly whisk the eggs, milk and vanilla together and gradually stir into the dry ingredients until they are just combined. Add the melted butter and stir until the mixture is smooth, but do not over-mix.

Pour the mixture into the prepared loaf tin and bake for 1 hour, or until the loaf is cooked – insert a skewer and if it comes out clean, then the bread is ready.

Leave the bread to cool in the tin for 5 minutes before removing to cool on a wire rack.

Cut into thick slices and then toast it and spread it with butter. Serve with the berry compote.

To make the berry compote

Melt the butter over a low heat in a pan, then stir in the sugar and vanilla extract and cook until the sugar melts. Tumble in your chosen berries, give the pan a good shake and continue to cook for 2–3 minutes until the fruit starts to soften.

Serve either warm or cold with the coconut bread dusted with sifted icing sugar, if using. You can refrigerate any leftover compote for a couple of days.

waffles – *with* chocolate *sauce &* toasted almonds

serves 6

Every breakfast book needs waffles. If you don't have a waffle iron, use a sandwich toaster; or, use the recipe to make yummy light pancakes.

For the waffles

- *300g / 10½oz / 2¼ cups plain flour*
- *1 tbsp corn flour*
- *4 tsp baking powder*
- *½ tsp salt*
- *2 tsp caster sugar*
- *2 large free-range eggs, separated*
- *120g / 4¼oz / 1 stick unsalted butter, melted*
- *400ml / 14fl oz / 1¾ cups whole milk*

For the chocolate sauce

- *225g / 8oz good plain chocolate, broken into pieces*
- *6 tbsp caster sugar*
- *120ml / 4fl oz / ½ cup double cream*
- *60ml / 2fl oz / ¼ cup hot water*

For the toasted almonds

- *100g / 3½oz / ⅞ cup flaked almonds*

To make the waffles
In a large mixing bowl, whisk together all the dry ingredients.

Beat the egg whites until moderately stiff and set aside.

Add the egg yolks, melted butter and milk to the dry ingredients and mix.

Fold the stiff egg whites into the mixture.

Ladle the mixture into a lightly greased hot waffle iron, close, and bake for approximately 5 minutes, or until golden and crisp. Be careful not to overfill.

When baked, keep the waffles warm on a cooling rack in a low oven. Don't stack them – lay them out individually.

If you do not have a waffle iron you can use a sandwich toaster to make a different shape.

To make the chocolate sauce
Put all the ingredients into a thick-bottomed saucepan. Put on a gentle heat and stir until the chocolate has melted and the sauce is hot.

To make the toasted almonds
Heat a small frying pan over a medium heat and add the flaked almonds, toss the almonds around until they become lightly golden. Remove from the heat and place the almonds into a dish.

Serve the waffles with a good spoonful of the warm chocolate sauce and a generous sprinkling of toasted almonds.

simple #4 pleasure

building a den

It really doesn't matter how young or old you are – everyone likes to have a little hideaway. You can build a den indoors, but nothing beats one made outdoors using nature's own building materials.

This is a team effort – gather your family or friends and build together. You're aiming for a ridge tent made with with trees and brushwood. You may need a saw.

1. Find a woodland and collect fallen branches – the longer they are, the roomier your den will be. You'll need:

- 1 x long pole for the ridge
- 8–20 short branches to make the sides. The longer the main pole, the more branches you'll need.

2. Balance the long pole up against a tree or a divide in a trunk. Lay the other end of the pole on the ground.

3. Lay the short poles perpendicular to the main pole, overlapping the branches to give good cover from the inside. The more you lay, the more robust your den will be. If you want to make your den watertight, you'll also need some rope and tarpaulin.

4. Find some evergreen fir and create a mat at the entrance to your den. Every time you walk in and out, the pine carpet will brush your shoes clean and release a lovely, fresh-pine aroma. Please be sensible and collect fallen branches only – and don't trespass.

Puddletown, Dorset

romantic mornings

serves 2

perfect *boiled* egg – *with* asparagus

A sophisticated twist on egg and soldiers and perfect for an early-summer breakfast in the garden. Just the two of you...

- *2 large free-range eggs, at room temperature*
- *1 bunch of asparagus*
- *sea salt and ground black pepper*

Place the eggs in a saucepan and add cold water to cover by 2.5cm / 1in. Bring to the boil over a medium-high heat. When the water boils, remove the pan from the heat and cover. Let the eggs stand like this for 4–5 minutes for a soft egg.

Using a slotted spoon, remove the eggs from the pan. If not using immediately, drain the hot water from the pan, fill with cold water and return the eggs to the pan to prevent further cooking.

Meanwhile, in a separate wide-rimmed pan, bring some salted water to the boil.

Prepare the asparagus by snapping off the woody ends (the ends will naturally break off from the tender part of the asparagus). Lay the asparagus in the pan of boiling water, bring back to the boil, and then reduce the heat to a simmer. Cook the asparagus for about 5 minutes, or until the stems are just tender. Drain.

Place each egg, pointed end down, in an egg cup on a plate and place some asparagus spears at the side. Serve immediately with salt and pepper.

serves 2

french toast – *with* passion fruit *curd*

Bring out your romantic side. This passion fruit curd marries perfectly with French toast and is utterly decadent. Make it for your better half and you can ask for anything...

For the passion fruit curd
- *11 passion fruit*
- *2 large free-range eggs*
- *2 large free-range egg yolks*
- *150g / 5½oz / ¾ cup caster sugar*
- *100g / 3½oz / scant 1 stick unsalted butter*

For the French toast
- *2 large free-range eggs*
- *4 tbsp whole milk*
- *1 tbsp caster sugar*
- *a few drops of good vanilla extract*
- *4 thick slices of white bread*
- *unsalted butter, for cooking*

To make the passion fruit curd
Remove the seeded pulp from 10 of the passion fruit and place in a food processor. Pulse a little just so the seeds loosen. Strain the juice into a jug and discard the seeds.

Beat the eggs, egg yolks and sugar together.

Melt the butter over a low heat in a heavy pan. When it has melted, stir in the egg and sugar mixture. Add the passion fruit juice and continue cooking, stirring constantly until thickened.

Off the heat, whisk in the seeded pulp from the remaining passion fruit. Cool slightly, then pour into a sterilised 350ml / 12fl oz jar (see page 178 for information on how to sterilise a jar).

This curd will keep in the refrigerator for up to 2 weeks.

To make the french toast
Mix together the eggs, milk, sugar and vanilla extract until the sugar has dissolved.

Dip the bread into the egg mixture so it is thoroughly coated. Fry slices in the butter until golden brown on both sides. Serve with the passion fruit curd.

serves 2

oeufs *en* cocotte

- *75g / 2½oz / ⅓ cup crème fraîche*
- *freshly grated nutmeg*
- *2 tbsp snipped fresh chives*
- *2 large free-range eggs*
- *sea salt and ground black pepper*

This classic French recipe is a simple dish of baked eggs. The name 'en cocotte' refers to the dishes in which the eggs are cooked. The following recipe is the basic method for baking the eggs in ramekins. There are several variations. For example, you could sprinkle a dessert spoon of grated Cheddar cheese on top of the cream. Other ingredients you could include under the egg are lightly cooked asparagus tips, or wilted leeks. You could also use chopped smoked salmon or lightly cooked flakes of smoked haddock.

Preheat the oven to 180°C / 350°F / Gas Mark 4.

Season the crème fraîche with a pinch of nutmeg, and salt and pepper to taste. Place a heaped tablespoon of crème fraîche in the bottom of a ramekin, followed by a sprinkling of chives, reserving a few for serving.

Crack an egg on top, then add a second tablespoon of crème fraîche and sprinkle with a pinch each of salt, pepper and nutmeg. Repeat with the other ramekin.

Place the ramekins in a baking dish and pour enough lukewarm water into the dish to come halfway up the sides of the ramekins.

Bake for 15 minutes, or until the egg yolks are set to your liking.

Dizzy

serves 2

smoked salmon eggs benedict

Smoked salmon is always a treat. People often worry about making hollandaise, but this method is really easy, and foolproof.

- *1 English muffin*
- *4 slices smoked salmon*

For the hollandaise sauce

- *160g / 5¾oz / 1½ sticks unsalted butter*
- *4 large free-range egg yolks*
- *3 tbsp freshly squeezed lemon juice*
- *sea salt & ground black pepper*

For the poached eggs

- *a good pinch of salt*
- *1 drop of malt vinegar or white wine vinegar (optional)*
- *2 large free-range eggs*

To make the hollandaise sauce
Melt the butter in a small saucepan.

Place the egg yolks and lemon juice in a blender and season with salt and pepper. Blitz for 15 seconds. With the blender running, slowly pour in the hot butter and blend for 30 seconds until the sauce is thick.

To poach the eggs
Half-fill a medium saucepan with water and bring to the boil. Add a hefty pinch of salt and the drop of vinegar (if using). Meanwhile, crack an egg into a small jug or bowl. Stir the boiling water vigorously with a balloon whisk until you have a whirlpool, then immediately slip the egg into the centre, lowering the jug 2cm / ¾in into the water. Turn the heat down low and cook for 3 minutes – use a timer to prevent overcooking.

Use a slotted spoon to scoop out the egg; then drain it on kitchen paper. Repeat for the other egg.

If you're poaching the eggs in advance, drop them straight into a bowl of iced water or they will carry on cooking. To reheat, simply warm the eggs through in a pan of gently simmering water.

Slice the muffin in half and toast. Spread some of the hollandaise on to a toasted muffin half and gently fold two smoked salmon slices on top of the sauce.

Top with a poached egg and gently spoon over some more hollandaise sauce. Sprinkle with black pepper. Repeat for the other muffin half.

serves 4

lemon *ricotta* pancakes – *with* raspberries

These pancakes are simply made for sharing. Keep them warm in the oven until you're ready to serve.

- *225g / 8oz / 1¾ cups plain flour*
- *1 tsp bicarbonate of soda*
- *½ tsp salt*
- *375ml / 13fl oz / 1⅔ cups buttermilk*
- *2 large free-range eggs, separated*
- *60g / 2¼oz / ⅓ cup caster sugar*
- *185g / 6½ oz / heaped ¾ cup ricotta cheese*
- *finely grated zest of ½ an unwaxed lemon*
- *2 tsp unsalted butter, melted*
- *1 punnet raspberries*
- *1 tbsp caster sugar (optional)*

Preheat the oven to 120°C / 250°F / Gas Mark ½.

In a large bowl, sift together the flour, bicarbonate of soda and salt.

In another bowl, whisk together the buttermilk, egg yolks, sugar, ricotta and lemon zest. Add the buttermilk mixture to the flour mixture and stir until just blended; there may be a few lumps.

In another bowl, whisk the egg whites until soft peaks form. Using a rubber spatula, carefully fold the egg whites into the batter until just blended.

Place a large griddle or frying pan over a medium heat until hot enough for a drop of water to sizzle and immediately evaporate.

Brush the griddle or pan with some of the melted butter. Put one ladleful of the batter into the hot pan. Reduce the heat to medium-low and cook until small bubbles appear on the surface of the pancake, the edges start to look dry and the bottoms golden brown, about 4 minutes.

Carefully turn the pancake over and cook until lightly browned on the other side, about 1½ minutes.

Transfer to an ovenproof platter and place in the oven to keep warm. Do not cover or your pancakes will get soggy! Repeat with the remaining butter and batter to make about 16 pancakes.

Serve with the raspberries, and sprinkled with sugar, if desired.

serves 4

blueberry & honey *bruschetta*

If you love blueberries, then you must try this recipe – the warm honey really brings out their flavour. Served over ice cream, blueberries and honey make a lovely dessert, too.

- *150ml / 5fl oz / 2/3 cup clear honey*
- *2 or 3 drops of good vanilla extract*
- *200g / 7oz / 1½ cups blueberries*
- *100g / 3½oz / scant ½ cup cream cheese or mascarpone*
- *half a baguette or sourdough bread, cut into 1.5cm / 5/8in slices*

In a small saucepan, bring the honey to the boil, remove from the heat and stir in the vanilla extract.

Put the blueberries in a heatproof bowl and pour over the honey mixture. Leave to stand for 5 minutes.

Whip the cream cheese or mascarpone just a little to make it lighter.

Toast the bread slices to your liking, then spread with some of the whipped cream cheese or mascarpone.

Put the toast on a serving plate and gently drizzle over the blueberry and honey mixture. Serve immediately. Delicious!

serves 2

chocolate & sea salt bagel *crisps*

Serve these posh toasts and pretend you're having a romantic weekend in Paris!

- *2 bagels, sliced horizontally in 5mm / ¼in slices*
- *100g / 3½oz thin plain chocolate with 70-per-cent cocoa solids*
- *extra virgin olive oil*
- *sea salt*

Preheat the oven to 180°C / 350°F / Gas Mark 4.

Lay the bagel slices on an ungreased baking tray and place thin squares of chocolate on each slice.

Pop the baking tray into the oven and bake only until the chocolate is melted but still holds its shape, about 1–2 minutes. Remove from the oven and immediately move the slices to a serving plate.

Sprinkle each slice with a few drops of the olive oil and then with a few flakes of sea salt – you're aiming to enhance the flavour of the chocolate – not to make it salty. Serve immediately.

serves 2

heart pancakes *– with* honey

There is nothing nicer than staying in bed when it's raining outside. These heart pancakes are kitsch, we know, but everyone loves a bit of old-fashioned romance. Make these for the love of your life. You'll need a heart-shaped metal cookie cutter.

- *3 large free-range eggs, separated*
- *115g / 4oz / heaped ¾ cup plain flour*
- *1 heaped tsp baking powder*
- *140ml / 4¾fl oz / ⅔ cup whole milk*
- *a pinch of salt*
- *4 tbsp clear honey, for drizzling*

Put the egg yolks in a large bowl and add the flour, baking powder and milk. Mix to a smooth, thick batter.

Whisk the egg whites with a pinch of salt until they form stiff peaks. Fold the whites into the batter.

Place a non-stick frying pan greased with vegetable oil on a medium heat. Place the cookie cutter into the pan, pour some of your batter into the cutter and fry for a couple of minutes until it starts to look golden and firm.

Loosen the pancake with a spatula, remove the cutter (take care not to burn yourself) and flip the pancake over. Continue cooking until both sides are golden. Remove the pancake and keep warm. Repeat until you have used up the remaining batter.

When all the pancakes are ready, divide them between two pretty plates and drizzle with the clear honey.

simple #5 pleasure

knitting

The ultimate simple pleasure is to make something for a loved one. Why not show your romantic side by knitting a scarf. It is surprisingly straightforward.

1. Visit your local craft or fabric shop and buy a set of knitting needles (size 8 / 4mm needles are good for your first attempt) and wool. Typically, you'll need three balls for a scarf, but more if you want an extra-long one.

2. Find one of the many great videos online of people showing you how to start to knit. You'll need just two basic stitches to start with – knit or garter and purl – as well as to learn how to cast on and off. You can find some great tips at craftyarncouncil.com

3. Make your first slip knot on one of the needles and you're ready to go, so turn off the TV and do something creative. Your loved one will be thrilled with their cosy scarf made with love come those chilly mornings!

Corfe Castle, Dorset

outdoors

serves 4

one pan breakfast

This is really easy to make and looks very impressive. It's also simple to substitute ingredients with whatever you've got to hand. Baby new potatoes are delicious; you can spice it up with some chorizo; or you can add a few peppers – there are endless variations. You can cook it on gas or an open fire. Everything tastes better outdoors.

- *olive oil*
- *2 medium potatoes, cubed, skin on*
- *1 onion, roughly chopped*
- *2 garlic cloves, crushed*
- *5 rashers of streaky or back bacon, roughly chopped*
- *a handful of cherry tomatoes*
- *about 10 closed cup mushrooms, roughly chopped*
- *leaves from 2 sprigs of fresh thyme*
- *4 large free-range eggs*
- *white or brown toast, to serve*
- *sea salt and ground black pepper*

Heat a little olive oil in a large non-stick frying pan. Add the potatoes, onion and garlic and fry over a medium heat for about 5 minutes. Add the bacon and continue to fry, stirring often, until the bacon is cooked and the potatoes are beginning to soften.

Add the tomatoes and mushrooms and simmer until the mushrooms are just soft and the tomato has been partially absorbed into the mixture. Add the thyme and season with salt and pepper, to taste.

With the back of a spoon, make 4 small hollows in the mixture. Carefully crack an egg into each hollow. Cover the pan with a lid and leave to cook until the eggs are as runny or as hard as you like; we cook it for only a minute or two, as we like runny egg yolks.

Serve with plenty of hot buttered toast.

serves
1

mushroom omelette

Some of the usual breakfast suspects captured in an omelette that's easy to prepare outdoors. Simple... but then the best things in life usually are.

- *2 tsp sunflower oil*
- *1 rasher of lean smoked bacon, chopped (optional)*
- *1 or 2 chestnut mushrooms, finely sliced*
- *1 tomato, sliced*
- *2 free-range eggs*
- *sea salt and ground black pepper*

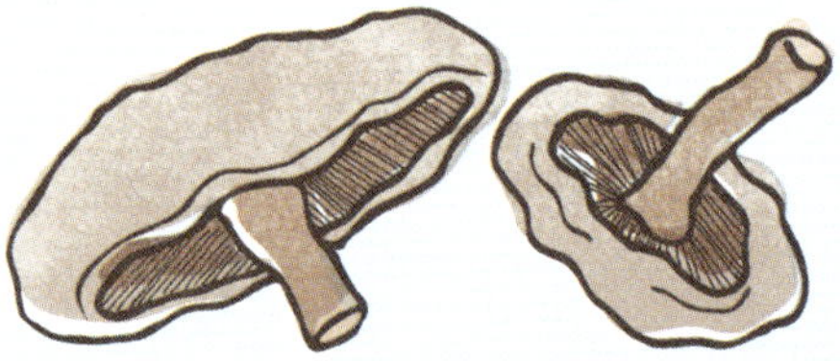

Brush a small non-stick frying pan lightly with 1 tsp sunflower oil. Heat the pan.

Once the pan is hot add the bacon, if using, mushrooms and tomato and cook for 2 minutes over a medium heat. When cooked remove from the pan and keep aside. Wipe the pan out and bush with the remaining sunflower oil.

Beat the eggs in a bowl with 2 teaspoons water and season with salt and pepper.

Heat the pan and when it is hot pour in the egg mixture and, using a wooden spoon, start to scramble the egg lightly. Turn down the heat, and spread the egg mixture smoothly to form an omelette; the egg does not need to be cooked thoroughly at this stage.

Place the cooked ingredients on top of the egg and cook over a low heat until the egg is almost set, 1 to 2 minutes. Slide the omelette carefully on to a plate. Invert the plate over the pan and release the omelette into the pan. Remove the plate. Continue to cook the omelette for another 1 – 2 minutes until golden underneath.

Remove from the heat and with a palette knife, or an egg slice, loosen the edges, fold in half and serve immediately.

Remove from the heat and with a palette knife, or an egg slice, loosen the edges, fold in half and serve immediately.

serves 4

mushrooms & campfire toast

Mushrooms always taste better when cooked with butter and salt. Using the olive oil as well ensures that the butter doesn't burn. This recipe really does capture the taste of the great outdoors!

- *1 tbsp olive oil*
- *2 tbsp salted butter*
- *8 field mushrooms, sliced*
- *2 garlic cloves, crushed*
- *4 slices farmhouse bread*
- *sea salt and ground black pepper*

Heat the oil and butter in a frying pan over the campfire. When sizzling, add the mushrooms and garlic. Continue cooking, stirring or shaking the pan so that the mushrooms cook evenly.

Meanwhile, toast the bread over the campfire. When the mushrooms wilt and soften they are ready.

Divide the mushrooms over the four pieces of toast and serve immediately.

serves 4

breakfast kebabs

Breakfast on the beach is one of our all-time favourite activities in Dorset. These kebabs are easy to prepare in advance. A simple bucket BBQ turns them into a delightful, smoky, cooked breakfast – perfect after that early morning swim.

- *8 rashers of back bacon*
- *1 red pepper, halved, deseeded and cut into chunks*
- *1 green pepper, halved, deseeded and cut into chunks*
- *1 yellow pepper, halved, deseeded and cut into chunks*
- *2 small red onions, cut into eighths*
- *8 cherry tomatoes*
- *16 small cocktail sausages*
- *8 wholemeal pitta breads or rolls, to serve*

Light a barbecue and wait until the coals burn grey and there are no flames before you begin to cook your kebabs.

Cut each rasher of bacon in half and roll up the halves to make them easier to thread onto skewers.

Thread the ingredients one by one on to eight wooden skewers, leaving a small gap between each piece. You can put the ingredients in any order, but make sure that each skewer has an equal amount of each ingredient.

Cook the kebabs over the fire or barbecue for about 15–20 minutes until golden and cooked through.

If you can, warm the pitta breads or rolls and serve with the kebabs.

serves 2

the ultimate sausage sandwich

Choose the best sausages and bread you can find – locally sourced if possible – and you'll be rewarded with one of the great breakfast experiences.

- *olive oil*
- *4 good pork sausages*
- *1 large onion, sliced*
- *1 tbsp balsamic vinegar*
- *1 tbsp Dijon mustard*
- *1 tbsp clear honey*
- *1 small ciabatta, split, halved and toasted*
- *tomato ketchup or brown sauce, to serve*

Heat a little olive oil in a heavy frying pan and cook the sausages on all sides for about 15 minutes, until cooked through. Remove the sausages from the pan and set aside. Add the onions to the pan, and cook until caramelised.

Stir in the balsamic, mustard and honey, and return the sausages to the pan to warm through. Pile into the ciabatta with the sauce of your choice.

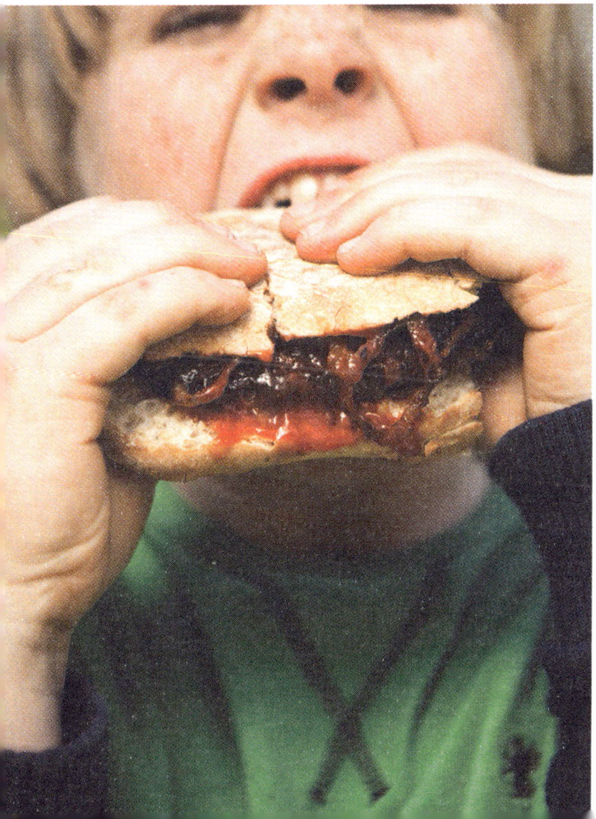
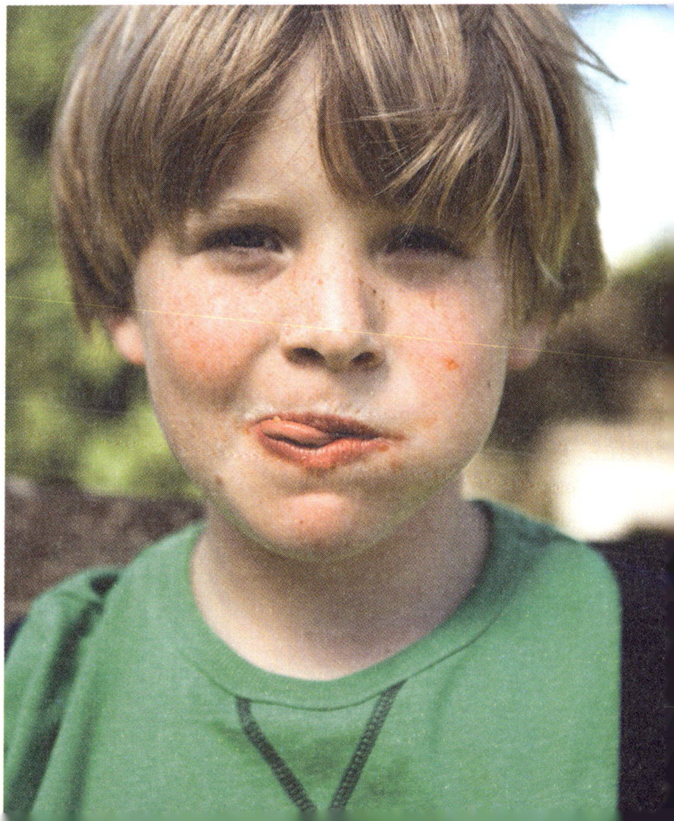

serves
2

cheesy *scrambled* eggs

Scrambled eggs with a cheesy twist – this is what toast was made for.

- *4 large free-range eggs*
- *8 tbsp single cream*
- *a knob of butter*
- *a large handful (100g / 3½oz) mature Cheddar cheese, grated*
- *1 tbsp good mayonnaise*
- *sea salt and ground black pepper*

Lightly whisk the eggs, cream and a pinch of salt and pepper together until just combined.

Heat a non-stick frying pan over a low heat for 1 minute or so, then add the butter and let it melt. Don't allow it to brown or it will discolour the eggs. Pour in the egg mixture and let it sit without stirring, for 20 seconds. Then, stir with a wooden spoon, lifting and folding it over from the bottom of the pan. Let it sit for another 10 seconds, then stir and fold again. Be careful not to over-stir.

Repeat until the eggs are softly set and slightly runny in places, then add the grated cheese and stir gently. Remove from the heat and leave for a few seconds to finish cooking.

Add the mayonnaise with a final stir and serve immediately on toast.

serves 1–10

granola *fruit* kebabs

Get your five a day in one hit from this fun-filled, outdoorsy breakfast. This is a great way to get your fellow campers together after a night under canvas.

- *strawberries, hulled*
- *apples, cored and cut into chunks*
- *pineapple, peeled, cored and cut into chunks*
- *melon, peeled, deseeded and cut into chunks*
- *cherries, halved and pitted*
- *grapes*
- *natural or flavoured yoghurt*
- *clear honey*
- *Dorset Cereals Honey Granola*

Prepare your fruits and place them in bowls, alongside a bowl each for the yoghurt, honey and granola.

Give each person a wooden skewer to spear their own choice of fruit.

Dunk the skewer in the yoghurt followed by the granola and honey before eating.

Remember – no double dipping!

the perfect camp fire

simple #6 pleasure

Puddletown, Dorset

No camping trip is complete without a roaring fire – although make sure you are permitted to light one. But making a really good one isn't just a matter of throwing on a few logs. Here's how we do it.

1. Roll up some balls of newspaper and put them in your fire pit. Make sure they are completely dry.

2. Surround the newspaper with a teepee of kindling sticks, pushing the bottom end of each stick firmly into the ground.

3. Around this, arrange a larger teepee of small logs.

4. Light the newspaper, stand back and enjoy the ultimate campfire.

Mudeford, Dorset

takeaway

makes
4

croque monsieur

Have a little continental walk to work this morning with a lovely croque monsieur – a heavenly mix of cheese, ham and mustard. Wrap it in greaseproof paper and off to work you go...

- *30g / 1oz / 2 tbsp unsalted butter*
- *2 tbsp plain flour*
- *350ml / 12fl oz / 1½ cups whole milk*
- *50g / 1¾oz Parmesan cheese, grated*
- *150g / 5½oz Gruyère cheese, grated*
- *8 slices good white bread*
- *Dijon mustard, to taste*
- *4 thick slices good ready-to-eat ham*
- *sea salt and ground black pepper*

Preheat the oven to 200°C / 400°F / Gas Mark 6.

Melt the butter in a saucepan over a medium-low heat. Add the flour and cook, stirring continuously, for about 2 minutes. Slowly add the milk, whisking all the time until the sauce thickens. Remove from the heat and season with salt and pepper. Add the Parmesan and 50g / 1¾oz / ½ cup of the Gruyère.

Place the bread on to a baking tray and toast in the oven for a few minutes on each side. Lightly spread some Dijon mustard on 4 slices of the toast, layer with the ham slices and sprinkle with another 50g / 1¾oz / ½ cup Gruyère. Top with the remaining slices of toast.

Spoon the sauce on the top of the sandwiches and sprinkle with the remaining Gruyère. Bake in the oven for 5 minutes, then finish off under the medium-hot grill until the tops are bubbling and lightly browned.

makes 9

baked berry tortilla

Feel free to choose your own Dorset Cereals favourite for this breakfast in a bar; we've used Berries & Cherries Muesli, which works a treat.

- *1 sachet Dorset Cereals Proper Porridge*
- *150g / 5½oz / 1½ cups Dorset Cereals Berries & Cherries Muesli*
- *275ml / 9½fl oz / 1¼ cups whole milk*
- *1 large free-range egg*
- *½ tsp good vanilla extract*

Preheat the oven to 180°C / 350°F / Gas Mark 4.

Mix the dry ingredients in one bowl and beat the wet ingredients in another. Put the contents of the two bowls together and stir to combine.

Pour the mixture into a 23cm / 9in square baking tray, lightly coated with vegetable oil or lined with baking parchment. Bake for 35 minutes, allow to cool, and cut into 9 squares. The bars will keep for up to 3 days in an airtight container.

Basil

makes 12

berries *& cherries* muffins

Natural, homemade muffins at a fraction of the cost of those at your local coffee shop. Make a batch of these on a Sunday night, keep one wrapped and ready for Monday morning, then freeze the rest. Each night, take one out to defrost – homemade muffins every morning. Yum!

- *200g / 7oz / 1½ cups plain flour*
- *2 tsp baking powder*
- *a pinch of salt*
- *125g / 4½oz / 1¼ cups Dorset Cereals Berries & Cherries Muesli*
- *230g / 8oz / 1 cup natural yoghurt*
- *1 large free-range egg, beaten*
- *90g / 3¼oz / scant ½ cup light brown sugar*
- *80ml / 2½fl oz / ⅓ cup vegetable oil*

Preheat the oven to 180°C / 350°F / Gas Mark 4. Place 12 muffin cases in a muffin tin.

Sift the flour, baking powder and salt together in a large bowl. In another bowl, mix the muesli and yoghurt, then add the egg, sugar and oil and stir to combine. Add the wet mixture to the dry mixture and stir until just combined.

Divide the mixture into the muffin cases and bake for about 20 minutes, or more if needed. The muffins are ready when a skewer comes out cleanly.

Bumble

fantastically fruity *twist* bread

serves 4

Show off your baking skills with this delicious bread.

For the bread

- *2 large free-range eggs, plus 2 egg whites*
- *100g / 3½oz / 1 cup Dorset Cereals Fantastically Fruity Muesli*
- *380g / 13½oz / 2⅞ cups plain flour*
- *3 tsp baking powder*
- *a pinch of salt*
- *70g / 2½oz / 5 tbsp caster sugar*
- *70g / 2½oz / 5 tbsp unsalted butter, chilled and cubed*
- *190ml / 6½fl oz / heaped ¾ cup whole milk*
- *2½ tbsp apricot jam*

For the icing (optional)

- *250g / 9oz / 1⅞ cups icing sugar*
- *zest of 1 unwaxed lemon*
- *1 tsp unsalted butter*
- *6 tbsp hot water*

To make the bread

Preheat the oven to 190°C / 375°F / Gas Mark 5.

Lightly whisk the egg whites until frothy. Put the muesli into a bowl and gently stir in the egg whites. Set aside for the filling.

Sift together the flour, baking powder and salt in a bowl then mix in the sugar. Rub in the butter until the mix resembles breadcrumbs. Whisk the eggs and milk together lightly and pour into the dry mixture, reserving a little for an egg wash. Combine, then knead for 30 seconds. Cut into 2 equal pieces.

Roll each piece into a 25cm / 10in square. Spread half the filling over each square, leaving 2cm / ¾in along one edge, and brush this edge with the egg wash.

Starting on the edge opposite the egg wash, roll up the dough and filling and secure closed with the egg-washed edge. Repeat for the other square of dough.

Place both rolls on a lined baking tray. Cut both in half lengthways, leaving 2cm / ¾in uncut at the top. Twist the 2 lengths together, securing them together at the end. Brush with egg wash and bake for 30 minutes.

Make a glaze by melting the jam and 50ml / 1¾fl oz water in a small pan over a low heat. Strain through a sieve if necessary and set aside. When the bread is out of the oven, brush with the glaze; leave to cool.

To make the icing (optional)

Beat the icing sugar, lemon zest, butter and water together until smooth. When the bread is cool, drizzle the icing over the top.

serves 4

chorizo, tomato & manchego *panini*

Add a little Spanish-flavoured sunshine to an ordinary panini – so much more delicious than something you buy in a sandwich shop...

- *1 ciabatta or baguette*
- *125ml / 4fl oz / ½ cup extra virgin olive oil*
- *125g / 4½oz / ½ cup cream cheese*
- *250g / 9oz ready-to-eat chorizo, finely sliced*
- *250g / 9oz Manchego cheese, finely sliced*
- *3 plum tomatoes, finely sliced*

Cut the bread crossways into 4 equal sections and then slice each section horizontally.

Brush the cut sides with about half the olive oil. Spread the bottom layers with the cream cheese, then the chorizo, followed by the Manchego. Finish with the sliced tomato and place the bread tops back on.

Heat a grill pan or heavy frying pan on a medium-high heat. Lightly brush the outsides of the sandwiches with the remaining olive oil. When the pan is hot, place 2 sandwiches into the pan and weigh down with another heavy pan (filled with 2 heavy cans). Cook for about 3 minutes until lightly browned.

Turn the sandwiches and weigh down again, then cook for another 3 minutes or so until the bottom is browned. Remove from the pan and keep warm while you cook the other 2 sandwiches.

serves 6

pancetta & tomato tarts

Take a little bit of deli deliciousness with you to nibble at on the move.

- *200g / 7oz pancetta slices, cubed*
- *2 garlic cloves, crushed*
- *leaves from 4 sprigs of fresh thyme*
- *400g / 14oz cherry tomatoes, halved*
- *60ml / 2fl oz / ¼ cup extra virgin olive oil, plus extra for drizzling*
- *1 x 500g / 1lb 2oz block ready-to-roll puff pastry*
- *150g / 5½oz soft goat's cheese*
- *125ml / 4fl oz / ½ cup whole milk*
- *sea salt and ground black pepper*

Preheat the oven to 200°C / 400°F / Gas Mark 6.

Heat a small frying pan over a medium heat, add the diced pancetta and cook for 3–4 minutes until the edges turn golden. Remove from the heat and drain on kitchen paper.

In a small bowl combine the garlic, thyme, tomatoes and olive oil. Season with salt and pepper and mix gently, then set aside.

On a lightly floured surface, roll out the puff pastry to ½cm / ¼in thick. Cut into 6 rectangles and place these on a baking sheet. Prick all over with a fork and bake for 10–12 minutes until light golden brown. Remove from the oven.

In another small bowl, use a fork to mix the goat's cheese with enough of the milk to achieve a spreading consistency (you may not need all the milk). Gently spread a heaped tablespoon of the goat's cheese mixture on to each pastry rectangle. Sprinkle over the cooked pancetta followed by the seasoned cherry tomatoes.

Bake until the tarts are warmed through, about 5–10 minutes. Drizzle with a little olive oil, season and serve.

makes 16

nutty cranberry *cinnamon* rolls

Make the office jealous when you rock up with one of these. Or bring a tray in for everyone to share... how to win friends and influence people.

For the rolls

- *900g / 2lb / 6½ cups strong white flour, sieved*
- *75g / 2½oz / heaped ½ cup dried cranberries*
- *2 tsp fast-acting yeast*
- *1 tsp salt*
- *3 tbsp caster sugar*
- *300ml / 10½fl oz / 1¼ cups tepid whole milk and 300ml / 10½fl oz / 1¼ cups tepid water, combined*
- *50g / 1¾oz / 3½ tbsp unsalted butter, softened*
- *100g / 3½oz / ½ cup light brown sugar*
- *2 tsp ground cinnamon*
- *100g / 3½oz / 1 cup Dorset Cereals Simply Nutty or Gloriously Nutty Muesli*

For the icing

- *300g / 10½oz / heaped 2 cups icing sugar*
- *2 tbsp maple syrup*
- *1 tsp good vanilla extract*
- *a little just-boiled water*

To make the rolls

To make in a mixer, place the flour, cranberries, yeast, salt and sugar in the mixer bowl, and fit with the dough hook. Add the warm milk and water with the machine running on a low speed. Continue mixing for 5 minutes. Remove the bowl, cover, and leave in a warm place until the dough is doubled in size, about 1½ hours.

To mix by hand, mix the dry ingredients in a large bowl and add the milk and water. Using your hands, mix well. Transfer to a floured surface and knead for 10 minutes, return to a clean bowl and leave to prove as above.

Tip on to a floured surface and knead lightly; you don't want to knock out the air. When the dough has a smooth appearance, roll it out into a 60cm / 24in square.

Spread the butter on the dough, right to the edges. Mix the brown sugar and cinnamon and sprinkle this over the butter – again, right to the edges. Now sprinkle over the muesli.

Roll up the dough into a Swiss roll, keeping it tight and even. Then slice into 16 equal slices.

Turn the sliced rolls over to expose the swirl. Place all 16 on a lined baking tray, leaving a small space between each roll. Cover loosely with another piece of baking parchment and put in a warm place for an hour.

Meanwhile, preheat the oven to 200°C / 400°F / Gas Mark 6. Bake the rolls for 15 minutes until golden brown.

To make the icing
Sieve the icing sugar, then add the maple syrup and vanilla extract with enough just-boiled water to make a thick but pourable icing. As soon as the rolls come out of the oven, drizzle over the icing.

Tear apart and enjoy!

makes 16

breakfast bars

The easiest way to take your favourite Dorset Cereals muesli with you, wherever you go...

- *1 x 397g / 14oz can condensed milk*
- *600g / 1lb 5oz / 6 cups Dorset Cereals muesli (Simply Delicious, Gloriously Nutty, or your favourite)*

Preheat the oven to 130°C / 250°F / Gas Mark ½. Oil a 23cm x 33cm x 4cm / 9in x 13in x 1½in baking tin.

Warm the condensed milk in a large pan.

Put the muesli into a bowl and add the condensed milk. Using a rubber or wooden spatula, fold to distribute the muesli evenly through the liquid.

Spread the mixture into the baking tin and press down with the spatula to level the surface.

Bake for 1 hour. Remove from the oven and set aside for 15 minutes before cutting into sections to make 16 chunky bars. Let cool completely.

The bars will keep for up to 5 days in an airtight container.

simple #7 pleasure

flying a kite

Follow these simple steps to get your kite soaring. But please be aware of power lines, houses, other people and trees. Happy flying!

1. Pick a windy day, find an open space, and take a friend – it's easiest with two people.

2. Unwind between 6–20 metres / 19–65 feet of the line while your friend holds the kite.

3. Your friend should be facing into the wind. He or she then holds the kite into the wind and ensures the line is tight.

4. On your signal, your friend launches the kite into the sky and moves out of the way.
You might need to adjust your position to keep the kite in flight. Just let out the line to make the kite climb.

Wimborne, Dorset

comfort

serves 6-8

muesli loaf

If tea and toast is the ultimate comfort food, then this is the Dorset Cereals version. Make this simple loaf using our Simply Delicious Muesli – guaranteed to lift your heart with both its taste and its delicious aroma while it's baking. Serve the loaf sliced and toasted with lashings of real butter, and homemade jam (page 178).

- *200g / 7oz / 2 cups Dorset Cereals Simply Delicious Muesli*
- *400g / 14oz / 3 cups strong white bread flour*
- *1 tsp easy-bake yeast*
- *1 tsp sea salt*
- *250ml / 9fl oz / 1⅛ cups tepid water*
- *3 tbsp clear honey*
- *40g / 1½oz / 3 tbsp unsalted butter, melted*

Preheat the oven to 200°C / 400°F / Gas Mark 6.

Mix the muesli, flour, yeast and salt together in a large bowl. Mix the water, honey and melted butter together in a large jug.

Add the honey mixture to the flour mixture and combine. If you are using a mixer with a dough hook, mix for about 3–4 minutes. If you are mixing by hand, transfer the dough to a floured surface and knead for 10 minutes.

Put the dough in a lightly greased bowl and cover with a damp cloth. Leave for 45 minutes, or until doubled in size.

Knead the dough lightly and roll it into a loaf shape. Place it in a loaf tin, seam-side down. Bake in the oven for about 40 minutes until rich brown in colour.

Put on a wire rack to cool before slicing for toast.

serves 2

porridge *with* whisky & honey

Another great comforting breakfast. This time with a little added whisky – for medicinal purposes only!

- *2 sachets of Dorset Cereals Proper Porridge*
- *3 tbsp double cream, plus extra to serve*
- *250ml / 9fl oz / $1\frac{1}{8}$ cups whole milk*
- *a dash of good whisky*
- *2 tbsp clear honey*

Place the porridge oats, cream, milk, whisky and 1 tablespoon of honey in a small saucepan and cook over a gentle heat for 5–6 minutes until thickened and smooth.

To serve, pour the porridge into 2 bowls and drizzle with the rest of the honey and a little cream.

serves 6

baked bananas

When you want something soothing, these baked bananas are just the job. Some slicing, sprinkling and baking, then 20 minutes later a warm and tasty breakfast.

- *6 firm, ripe bananas*
- *45g / 1½oz / 3 tbsp unsalted butter*
- *3 tbsp freshly squeezed lemon juice*
- *3 tbsp brown sugar*
- *1 tsp cinnamon*
- *finely grated zest of 1 orange, to serve*
- *2 tbsp grated fresh coconut or desiccated coconut, to serve*

Preheat the oven to 180°C / 350°F / Gas Mark 4.

Peel the bananas and cut them into 6cm / 2½in chunks.

Place the butter and lemon juice in a shallow baking dish. Pop the dish into the oven until the butter melts and then add the bananas and coat with the butter mixture. In a small bowl, mix together the brown sugar and cinnamon and sprinkle this over the bananas.

Bake for 20 minutes, or until the bananas are heated through and the butter is just bubbling.

Serve sprinkled with orange zest and coconut.

serves 9

raspberry oatmeal *breakfast* cake

If you need an excuse to eat cake at breakfast, here it is.

- *150g / 5½oz / 1 heaped cup plain flour*
- *50g / 1¾oz / 6 tbsp wholewheat flour*
- *75g / 2½oz / ¾ cup Dorset Cereals Proper Raspberry Porridge or Oat and Barley Porridge*
- *75g / 2½oz / 6 tbsp caster sugar*
- *2 tsp baking powder*
- *¼ tsp salt*
- *170ml / 5½fl oz / scant ¾ cup skimmed milk*
- *50ml / 1¾fl oz / scant ¼ cup low-fat natural yoghurt*
- *1 large free-range egg*
- *2 tbsp cornflour*
- *175g / 6oz / 1½ cups fresh or partially thawed frozen raspberries*

Preheat the oven to 200°C / 400°F / Gas Mark 6.

In medium bowl, combine the two flours, oats, sugar, baking powder and salt.

In a separate smaller bowl, beat together the milk, yoghurt, egg and cornflour.

Add the combined wet ingredients to the combined dry ingredients and stir until just moistened. Fold in the raspberries.

Spoon the batter into a buttered and floured, non-stick 20cm / 8in square baking tin. Bake in the oven for 20–25 minutes until a toothpick or knife tip inserted in the centre comes out clean (except for maybe a little bit of blue from the berries).

Allow the cake to cool for at least 10 minutes before slicing into 9 squares.

serves 4-6

bircher muesli

The original muesli, and one you can make truly your own. Follow the recipe below, or use your imagination and taste buds to create your own favourite. Try different flavoured yoghurts – coconut flavour is lovely; use grated pear instead of apple for a gentler finish; add a hint of cinnamon or ginger to spice it up. This recipe is really nurturing for your body as well as your soul.

- *125g / 4½oz / heaped 1¼ cups rolled oats*
- *75g / 2½oz / heaped ½ cup raisins*
- *175ml / 5½fl oz / ¾ cup cloudy apple juice*
- *freshly squeezed juice of 1 lemon*
- *100ml / 3½fl oz / scant ½ cup natural yoghurt*
- *1 apple, peeled, cored and grated*
- *25g / 1oz / ¼ cup flaked almonds*
- *a handful of strawberries and blueberries, to serve*

Place the oats and raisins into a large dish; pour over the apple juice and the lemon juice. Cover with a clean, dry cloth and leave to soak overnight (in the refrigerator if the weather is hot).

When you are ready to serve, stir in the remaining ingredients and divide into bowls. Feel free to add some milk if you prefer a looser texture.

Delicious served with fresh berries in the summer, or a tangy fruit compote.

serves 4-6

boxty – *with* poached *eggs*

This is true comfort food in an Irish fashion. Two kinds of potato join to make little cakes that are a joy to eat with a softly poached egg.

For the boxty

- *500g / 1lb 2oz / 3¼ cups potatoes, peeled and grated*
- *500g / 1lb 2oz / 2¼ cups cold mashed potato*
- *420g / 15oz / scant 3¼ cups plain flour*
- *1 heaped tsp baking powder*
- *30g / 1oz/2 tbsp unsalted butter, melted*
- *200ml / 7fl oz / ⅞ cup whole milk*
- *1-2 tbsp olive oil*
- *sea salt and ground black pepper*

For the poached eggs

- *a pinch of salt*
- *4-6 large free-range eggs*
- *1 drop of malt vinegar or white wine vinegar (optional)*

To make the boxty

Wrap the grated potato in a clean tea towel and wring it well to get rid of any excess liquid.

Transfer the grated potato into a mixing bowl, add the cold mash and mix until combined.

Add the flour and baking powder and mix again until well combined. Stir in the melted butter and season to taste.

Add the milk, a little at a time, beating after each addition until it has been fully incorporated. You should have a mixture that resembles a thick, heavy batter. If the mixture is too sticky, add more milk as necessary. Set aside.

Meanwhile, heat the oil in a large, non-stick frying pan over a medium-high heat. Add spoonfuls of the batter, leaving space around each spoonful for the mixture to spread. Fry the boxties for 3–4 minutes on each side, or until golden brown and the potato is cooked through.

Remove the boxties from the pan using a slotted spoon, set aside to drain on kitchen paper, and keep warm. Repeat the process with the remaining boxty mixture.

To make the poached eggs

See the recipe for smoked salmon eggs benedict on page 108.

To serve, divide the boxties among 4–6 serving plates. Place a poached egg on top of each boxty.

homemade scones *– with* clementine *&* cinnamon butter

makes 10

Sometimes a bit of home baking is just the way to lift your mood – kitchen therapy, if you like. Make your own butter and use the buttermilk to make scones. Brilliant! Of course, you can use readymade buttermilk and beat the clementine, cinnamon and sugar into 200g / 7oz unsalted butter.

For the butter

- *570ml / 20fl oz / 2½ cups double cream*
- *finely grated zest of 1 clementine*
- *¼ tsp ground cinnamon*
- *70g / 2½ oz / 5 tbsp light brown sugar*

For the scones

- *225g / 8oz / 1¾ cups self-raising flour*
- *a pinch of salt*
- *50g / 1¾oz / 2 tbsp unsalted butter, chilled and cubed*
- *25g / 1oz / 2 tbsp caster sugar*
- *4 tbsp whole milk*

To make the butter

Pour the cream into a mixing bowl and, using an electric whisk, beat until it starts to look like it's curdling (it will turn a bit yellow). Continue beating – you'll see it separating and liquid coming out of the mixture. Pour off this buttermilk and set aside (you should have about 250ml / 9fl oz, some of which you can use to make the scones; see overleaf).

Begin beating again – the mixture will start to resemble butter and more buttermilk will come out; keep pouring it off. Once you have something that looks like butter, stop beating with the whisk and finish off with a wooden spoon. Keep pushing the butter about to remove any remaining liquid.

Hold the butter and run it under the cold tap until the water runs clear. Place it in a clean bowl and beat in the clementine zest, cinnamon and 4 tablespoons of the sugar. Taste; if you would like it a bit sweeter, add the remaining tablespoon of sugar.

To make the scones

Preheat the oven to 220°C / 425°F / Gas Mark 7 and lightly butter a baking tray (unless you're using a non-stick tray).

Tip the flour into a mixing bowl, along with the salt. Add the butter, then rub together with your fingers to make a reasonably fine-crumbed mixture, lifting to aerate the mixture as you go. Try not to over-rub, as the mixture will be lighter if it's a little bit flaky. Stir in the sugar.

Measure the buttermilk left over from making the batter, and then mix in the milk to slacken it. Make a well in the middle of the flour mixture with a round-bladed knife and pour in most of this buttermilk mixture, holding a little bit back – you may not need it all.

Using the knife, gently work the mixture together until it forms a soft, almost sticky dough. Work in any loose, dry bits of mixture with the remaining buttermilk, if needed. Don't overwork at this point or you'll toughen the dough.

Lift the ball of soft dough out of the bowl and put it on to a very lightly floured surface. Knead a little to remove any cracks.

Pat the dough gently with your hands to a thickness of no less than 3cm / 1¼in and no more than 4cm / 1½in. Dip a 5.5cm / 2¼in round, fluted cutter into a bowl of flour (this helps to stop the dough sticking to it), then cut out the scones by pushing down quickly and firmly on the cutter with the palm of your hand, but don't twist it. You will hear the dough give a big sigh as the cutter goes in. Gather the trimmings lightly, then pat and cut out a couple more scones.

Place the scones on the baking tray and sift over a light dusting of flour. Bake for 10–12 minutes until risen and golden.

Cool on a wire rack, uncovered if you prefer crisp tops, or covered loosely with a cloth for soft ones.

Serve with the clementine and cinnamon butter.

serves 3

hot chocolate *&* cinnamon *toast*

It's good to take the time to make proper hot chocolate – just look at your family's faces when they taste this.

For the hot chocolate

- *500ml / 17fl oz / 2 cups whole milk*
- *1 vanilla pod, split lengthways and deseeded*
- *75g / 2½oz plain chocolate with 70-per-cent cocoa solids, coarsely grated*
- *1 tbsp light or dark brown sugar*

For the cinnamon toast

- *3 slices good white bread*
- *50g / 1¾oz / 3 tbsp unsalted butter*
- *30g / 1oz / 2 heaped tbsp caster sugar*
- *1 tsp ground cinnamon*

To make the hot chocolate

Put the milk and the vanilla pod and seeds in a saucepan and place over a medium-low heat until it reaches a gentle simmer. Remove from the heat and allow the vanilla to infuse the milk, about 10–15 minutes.

Add the chocolate and sugar to the milk and whisk until they have melted. Return the pan to the heat, reduce the heat to low and cook until the chocolate is steaming but not boiling. Discard the vanilla pod and pour into the mugs. If you have any chocolate left over from the original bar, grate some over each mug.

To make the cinnamon toast

Toast both sides of the bread under a preheated grill.

Slather one side of each slice of toast with the butter, right up to the edges. Mix the caster sugar and cinnamon together and sprinkle over the buttered toast.

Return the toast to the grill for 2–3 minutes until the sugar begins to melt and bubble.

Serve immediately.

baked *roasted* hazelnut & ginger *oatmeal*

serves 6

This recipe has winter and comfort written all over it! Get it all ready, pop it into the oven and go for a short, brisk walk before returning home to the welcoming aroma of ginger and nuts and the promise of something rich and comforting to tuck into.

- *vegetable oil, for coating*
- *15g / ½oz / 1 tbsp unsalted butter*
- *3 large yellowish/green bananas, sliced*
- *1½ tsp ground cinnamon*
- *2 tbsp maple syrup*
- *165g / 5¾oz / 1¾ cups Dorset Cereals Gloriously Nutty Muesli*
- *12 tbsp glacé ginger, chopped*
- *50g / 1¾oz / ¼ cup brown sugar*
- *1 tsp baking powder*
- *1 tsp ground ginger*
- *360ml / 12½fl oz / 1½ cups whole milk*
- *1 large free-range egg, lightly beaten*
- *2 tbsp peeled and grated root ginger*
- *vanilla or natural yoghurt, to serve*

Preheat the oven to 190°C / 375°F / Gas Mark 5. Lightly coat a 20cm / 8in square baking dish or a 23cm / 9in round one with oil.

Melt the butter in a non-stick pan over a medium heat. Add the sliced bananas and cook for about 2 minutes, gently flipping to evenly brown both sides. Add 1 teaspoon of cinnamon and 1 tablespoon of maple syrup and let the mixture boil and thicken for about 30 seconds. Spoon the bananas into the bottom of the baking dish in an even layer. Set aside.

In a medium bowl, mix the muesli, glacé ginger, sugar, baking powder, ground ginger and remaining cinnamon. Set aside.

In a large bowl, whisk the milk, egg, root ginger and remaining tablespoon of maple syrup.

Stir the muesli mixture into the milk mixture, then pour it all over the bananas in the baking dish.

Bake for 15 minutes and then turn the oven up to 200°C / 400°F / Gas Mark 6 and bake for another 15 minutes until the top is slightly crisp and browned.

Allow to cool for a few minutes. Serve with a dollop of vanilla or natural yoghurt.

makes 8-10

pain *au* raisin

French comfort food in all its glory – enjoy this with a big cup of milky coffee. Get the pastries ready the evening before and leave them to rise slowly in the fridge overnight. Then, all you have to do is pop them into the oven in the morning.

For the starter

- *1 tsp fast-acting yeast*
- *75ml / 2½fl / ⅓ cup oz tepid water*
- *50g / 1¾oz / heaped ⅓ cup strong white bread flour*

For the dough

- *75ml / 2½fl oz / ⅓ cup cold whole milk*
- *-1 free-range egg, beaten, plus 2 yolks*
- *50ml / 1½fl oz / 3 tbsp double cream, chilled*
- *25g / 1oz/2 tbsp caster sugar*
- *250g / 9oz / 2⅛ sticks unsalted butter, chilled and cubed*
- *300g / 10½oz / 2 heaped cups strong white bread flour, plus extra for rolling*
- *1 tsp salt*
- *100g / 3½oz / ¾ cup raisins*

To make the starter
In a warm bowl, dissolve the yeast in the warm water, beat in the flour until smooth, cover, and leave for 20 minutes to bubble.

To make the dough
Whisk the milk, egg yolks, cream and sugar into the yeast mixture. Add the butter cubes and then the flour and salt. Stir everything together to form a rough, lumpy dough. Scoop it out on to a floured worktop and roll out until 1cm / ½in thick.

Fold it into thirds, then roll it out as before. Fold it in by thirds again, then wrap and chill for 30 minutes. Repeat this rolling and chilling sequence twice more.

Halve the dough, then roll each piece to 30cm x 15cm x 1cm / 12in x 6in x ½in. Brush the surface with water and generously dot with the raisins. Roll tightly up along the length, so you have a short, fat scroll. Seal the end with water, then cut into 4 wheels. Repeat until you have used all the dough.

Line a baking tray with baking parchment and put the prepared pastries on top. (You may need more than one tray.) Cover loosely with cling film and leave to rise in a warm place until almost doubled in size.

Once risen, brush with beaten egg and bake at 200°C / 400°F /Gas Mark 6 for 10 minutes. Lower the heat to 180°C / 350°F / Gas Mark 4 and bake for another 15–20 minutes, until crisp and golden.

simple #8 pleasure

homemade jam

No jam is as heavenly as one made using berries you've chosen yourself and turned into sweet nectar in your own kitchen. It is so simple.

1. For three 450g / 1lb jars, you will need:

- 900g / 32oz/ 2lb fresh or frozen berries
- 900g / 32oz/ 2lb white sugar, warmed in a stainless-steel bowl in a medium oven for 15 minutes.

2. Wash and dry your jam jars, then sterilise them by putting them in an oven set at 150°C / 300°F / Gas Mark 2 for 15 minutes.

3. Put the berries in a wide, stainless-steel saucepan. Mash them a little and cook for 3–4 minutes over a medium heat until the juices begin to run. Add the warmed sugar and stir over a gentle heat until it is fully dissolved.

4. Increase the heat, bring the mixture to the boil and cook for 5–6 minutes, stirring frequently.

5. Test to see if the jam will set: put 1 teaspoon of the jam on a cold plate and leave it for a few minutes in a cool place. Press with your index finger. If it wrinkles even slightly, it is set. Remove from the heat immediately. Skim and pour into the jars. Cover.

Christchurch Harbour, Dorset

Directory

Some of our favourite breakfast friends:
Riverford Organics riverford.co.uk

Cornish Sea Salt cornishseasalt.co.uk

Samways Fish samwaysfish.com

Pipers Farm pipersfarm.com

Chesil Smokery chesilsmokery.com

Yeo Valley yeovalley.co.uk

The Tomato Stall thetomatostall.co.uk

Dorset Down Mushrooms

Dorset Blue Viney cheese dorsetblue.com

Rowse Honey for wonderful honey rowsehoney.co.uk

And the Dorset Famous Five:
dorsetfamousfive.co.uk

Clipper teas for their amazing tea clipper-teas.com

Denhay bacon for the most delicious bacon in the UK denhay.co.uk

Olives et Al for their fantastic food, delis and eateries olivesetal.co.uk

Hall & Woodhouse for great beers hall-woodhouse.co.uk

And ourselves!

There are some lovely things we like using in our kitchen, too:
Cornishware tggreen.co.uk

Aebleskiver pans – you can find a selection of these at amazon.co.uk

Wüsthof Knives wusthofknives.co.uk

Keith Brymer Jones homeware keithbrymerjones.com

Williams-Sonoma cookware and tableware (OK, they're not British, but we love them!) williams-sonoma.com

Our simple pleasure friends:
Woodworking and crafty camping mallinson.co.uk

Our friends at River Cottage HQ rivercottage.net

Mushroom foraging courses at The Olive Tree Cookery School olivetreecookeryschool.com

Grow your own salad and vegetable gardens rocketgardens.co.uk

Hive Beach Café for amazing food and a stunning location hivebeachcafe.co.uk

For camping with soul, it's got to be a bell tent belltent.co.uk

And to find out a lot more about Dorset get hold of a copy of *The Little Book of Dorset* by Emma Mansfield (Lovely Little Books, 2011).

Index

Acknowledgements

So many people have helped make this book possible and we would like to thank each and everyone of them.

Firstly, the entire Dorset Cereals team who have provided inspiration, support and good humour in helping out with this book, including appearing in shoots, testing and eating the recipes (well, someone has to!) – thank you all. Your hard work, enthusiasm and dedication to excellence in everything Dorset Cereals does and creates is inspiring.

We would also like to thank Caroline Harris and Clive Wilson from Harris + Wilson for their hard work, creativity, attention to detail, and endless enthusiasm; our publisher Rebecca Spry at Anova Books for her total support for the project and boundless energy; designers Ross Imms and Luke Wright from A-Side Studio for their patience, good humour and the wonderful illustrations; Vicki Savage for her food styling; Pene Parker for her art direction; Big Fish for pack design and additional graphics.

For the wonderful photos we want to thank James Bowden, our photographer, who has taken so many beautiful images we can't fit them all in the book; and Jonathan Cherry for additional photography.

And a huge thank you to everyone else who helped make this book happen including Vicky and Jessica Shaw; Jeremy, Milly and Barnaby Barnes and their dog Bumble; Simon and Daniel Best; William Bilbe-Smith; Vanessa, Nick, Ollie, Tibbs and Patrick Morris and their dog Smartie; Dizzy Crankshaw, Ronnie Brown, Dawn Rolls and Jenny Pearce for the loan of their Weymouth beach hut; Gemma Hendicott, John Patterson and Tess Bush for the use of their Mudeford beach hut; Amelia Skinner of Phillips & Skinner in Bruton; John, Charlotte and Alex Ashfield; John and Suzanne Deverell, and the team at Positive PR, Sherborne, Dorset.

Harris + Wilson would also like to thank James Aiken, Judy Barratt, Vanessa Bird, Lucy Cox, Lee Faber, Yvonne and Peter Henness, Paul Humber, Jane Middleton, Vicky Millar, Jenni Moore, Kate Robinson, Hannah Stocks, Emma and Luca Stocks.

This book is dedicated to everyone who has ever bought a box of Dorset Cereals and for anybody who is yet to... Enjoy x

A little bit about us

Dorset Cereals award-winning breakfast cereals are created in Poundbury, Dorset and are all made to recipes which are packed with goodness – Mueslis, Granolas, Porridges, Flakes and Cereal Bars.

Dorset Cereals has been awarded numerous Gold medals for taste, design and packaging which reflect the uncompromising dedication the company has to making premium cereals. The company was voted runner-up in Sainsbury's Magazine's 2010 Brand of the Decade. They have also been nominated twice for the UK's top 500 Cool Brands.

Dorset Cereals has long been a supporter of The Woodland Trust and has sponsored the planting of 16,000 trees across the UK as part of the Jubilee Woods project. They, along with local residents have planted their own woodland of 1,000 trees near their HQ at Poundbury, Dorset.

For more simple pleasures and things to win and do visit us at dorsetcereals.co.uk

Dorset Cereals
Peverell Avenue East
Poundbury
Dorset, DT1 3WE

Cheryl Bouchier, our Dorset Cereals development chef, coming up with another fantastic recipe...

This edition first published in the United Kingdom in 2014 by National Trust Books

An imprint of Pavilion Books Company Ltd
1 Gower Street, London WC1E 6HD

First published in 2013 by Pavilion Books

Additional photography: Jonathan Cherry (p.11 *bottom right*, p.21, p.33, p.103, p.111, p.145, p.188); Big Fish (p.180–181); © shutterstock (p.118–119); and the following contributors to the Simple Pleasures photo competition: Ellen Birch (p.19 *top left*); Emma Gutteridge (p.19 *middle left*); Mary-Anne Reddaway (p.19 *top right*)

ISBN 9781909881341

A CIP catalogue record for this book is available from the British Library.

10 9 8 7 6 5 4 3 2 1

Repro by Rival Colour Ltd, UK
Printed by LEGO, S.p.A, Italy

This book can be ordered direct from the publisher at www.pavilionbooks.com, or try your local bookshop.
Also available at National Trust shops or www.nationaltrust.org.uk/shop

Cook's note: both metric and imperial measures are given for the recipes. Follow either set of measures, not a mixture of both, as they are not interchangeable. Medium eggs should be used except where otherwise specified. Free-range eggs are recommended. Recipes containing raw eggs are unsuitable for pregnant women and young children.

MIX
Paper from responsible sources
FSC® C023419